THE
REFERENCE
SHELF

POLAND

edited by WILLIAM P. LINEBERRY

THE REFERENCE SHELF

Volume 56 Number 2

THE H. W. WILSON COMPANY

New York   1984

094829

THE REFERENCE SHELF

The books in this series contain reprints of articles, excerpts from books, and addresses on current issues and social trends in the United States and other countries. There are six separately bound numbers in each volume, all of which are generally published in the same calendar year. One number is a collection of recent speeches; each of the others is devoted to a single subject and gives background information and discussion from various points of view, concluding with a comprehensive bibliography. Books in the series may be purchased individually or on subscription.

Library of Congress Cataloging in Publication Data

Main entry under title:

Poland.

    (The Reference shelf ; v. 56, no. 2)
    1. Poland—History—1980-   . I. Lineberry,
William P.   II. Series.
DK4442.P58   1984   943.8´056   84–11977
ISBN 0-8242-0697-5

Printed in the United States of America

CONTENTS

PREFACE

By the spring of 1984 the dramatic events in Poland that seemed to presage nothing less than a revolution within the Soviet bloc, had faded from the headlines. In place of the exultation and sense of long-awaited freedom that had accompanied the rise of the Solidarity trade union movement, a mood of passive, sullen resignation now prevailed. Despite occasional outbursts of protest, the most recent caused by the government's attempt to remove Christian icons from school classrooms, Poland again knows the uneasy calm enforced by a police state, while out of sight of Western reporters the three main forces in Polish society—workers, Catholic church and government—struggle to set the country and its ailing economy to rights.

Although the hopes of the Polish workers were dashed by the imposition of martial law, the events of 1980 and 1981, the latest in Poland's long and tormented history, will not soon be forgotten by Poles, their Communist neighbors, or the members of the Western alliance. For the first time in post-World War II history, a totalitarian Communist regime was forced to negotiate with a people's movement that, in defiance of Marxist-Leninist doctrine, refused to obey the orders of the government and insisted that it grant legal recognition to an independent trade union. The chain of events that began on July 1, 1980 with a series of unrelated strikes prompted by rising food prices reached a climax in August 1981, when Solidarity, having won every conflict with the government and claiming the right to speak for the Polish people, decided to modify its policy of direct confrontation and consolidate the gains it had won. Said the union's leader, Lech Walesa: "Let the government govern the country and we will govern ourselves in the factories."

The principle of collective bargaining, however, could not be accepted by General Wojciech Jaruzelski, who replaced Stanislaw Kania as head of state in October 1981, imposed martial law, and destroyed Solidarity by jailing its leaders. Despite the moral support offered by the Catholic church and its Polish leader, Pope

John Paul II, and by the Western world, whose sympathy for this workers' revolt against a workers' state was aptly symbolized by Lech Walesa's 1983 Nobel Prize for Peace, Polish workers have not, except in a few sporadic and bloody confrontations, challenged the authority of the new military regime, whose power is confirmed by the presence of Soviet armored divisions to the East, and East German ones to the West. Poles seem rather to be following the advice given them more than two centuries ago by Jean-Jacques Rousseau: "Poles!, if you cannot prevent your neighbors from devouring your nation, make it impossible for them to digest it."

The conditions in Poland that led to the uprising of 1980 were, as the second section of this compilation makes clear, the direct outcome of close economic ties that Poland had forged during the 1970s with several Western governments, notably West Germany and the United States. While officials in Bonn and Washington applauded the rise of Solidarity, it quickly became clear that the growth of democratic institutions in a Communist country presented a threat to the stability of Europe, and perhaps to the whole world. When threatened by a Hungarian uprising in 1956, and the popularity of a liberal Czechoslovakian government in 1968, the Soviets had preserved the integrity of their dominions by force. The threat of an independent Poland was even more serious since, as several articles reprinted here explain, the country plays a principal military role in the Warsaw pact and is tied economically to the U.S.S.R. more firmly than it is to the West. As Russians tanks massed along the Polish border, the crisis posed a challenge to diplomacy that no Western nation was able to meet. The difficulty was resolved—at least temporarily—by a development that no-one had predicted: under General Jaruzelski's orders, the Polish army, in a swift overnight exercise, seized control of the nation on December 13, 1981, thus finding a Polish solution to the crisis that Polish nationalism, with its strong element of anti-Soviet feeling, had caused. Although the U.S. and many of its allies protested by imposing economic sanctions, there were signs that some European governments, and numerous banks which had made massive unsecured loans to Poland during the 1970s, were not sorry to see the return of business as usual.

The questions that arose from the turmoil of the early 1980s have not, however, been settled, and the drama of Poland's internal conflict has not been played out. An uneasy political truce prevails, and Poland's dire economic problems remain unsolved. The future is a large question mark, and the purpose of this volume is to provide a historical, political, and economic sketch of the circumstances that inform that doubt. The first section describes the historical background, the rise of Solidarity, and the economic conditions that did much to provoke the crisis. The second section concentrates on Poland's international importance and poses the question of how the West should respond to events that threaten the stability of its political adversary. The third section describes Poland in the aftermath of martial law, presenting a picture of a population aware of its own power, but uncertain of how to use it.

The editor wishes to thank those authors and publishers who have kindly granted permission to reprint the material in this compilation.

William P. Lineberry

April 1984

I. BACKGROUND TO A POLISH TRAGEDY

EDITOR'S INTRODUCTION

No European nation has been fought over more savagely or more frequently than Poland, and no European people has a stronger sense of nationhood than the Poles. As William E. Schaufele, Jr. a former U.S. Ambassador to Poland, writes in the first article in this section, "Poland has had moments of glory and tragedy, of empire and obliteration, of freedom and occupation, of independence and partition, but the Polish nation has never lost its identity or its vigor."

Certainly, Polish nationalism played a crucial part in the emergence of an independent union that, with 10 million members, could justifiably claim to have supplanted the Polish Communist Party as the voice of the people. Popular risings had occurred in Poland in 1956, 1970, and 1976, but all were quickly suppressed by the government, who avoided prolonged tension by rescinding price increases, thus, ironically, preparing the ground for the economic crisis that brought political discontent to a head in 1980. By the time Lech Walesa, in mid-1980, began the show of quiet, nonviolent resistance in a Gdansk shipyard, all sectors of Polish society excepting the ruling hierarchy were ready to act in concert and did so with a conviction that made Solidarity and Walesa seemingly invincible. Another factor in the rise of Polish nationalism was the election of Karol Wojtyla to the Papacy in 1978. Now that the Catholic Church, long the defender of Polish liberties, had a Polish leader, it could not help but seem to many workers that God was on their side. But the discontent had other, nonspiritual causes. Inflation, an insupportable national debt, and a decade of corrupt, inefficient management had created the conditions for revolution.

The three articles in this section trace the three principal strands in Polish history that came together in 1980: former Ambassador Shaufele surveys 1,000 years of Polish history, explaining how the government lost its hold on the people. John Darnton, the *New York Times* Warsaw bureau chief, charts the rise of Solidarity in the context of Polish social conditions, and an article from *Fortune* describes the economic conditions that destroyed the credibility of the government.

POLISH PARADOX:
COMMUNISM AND NATIONAL RENEWAL[1]

Describing Poland after its partition among three other powers in the 18th century, an English historian stated, "The nation existed without a state." All countries and their peoples are products of their particular history, geography, culture and all the other factors which combine to make up the contemporary nation-state. Poland is no exception and, in many ways, the concept of "nation" as distinct from "state" is stronger there than in most countries.

Throughout its history of over 1,000 years, Poland has had moments of glory and tragedy, of empire and obliteration, of freedom and occupation, of independence and partition, but the Polish nation has never lost its identity or its vigor. It has been the victim of contending princes and dukes, kings and czars, fuehrers and commissars. Its borders have extended as far east as Kiev, the capital of Soviet Ukraine, as far south as the Black Sea, as far west as the Oder river and as far north as the Gulf of Riga. It has been invaded by the Mongols, Prussians, Swedes, Austrians, Nazi Germans, and both Czarist and Soviet Russians. In the 18th century it was subjected to three successive partitions involving Prussia, Russia and Austria and reemerged as an independent state after World War I only to be invaded and partitioned once more by Nazi Germany and the Soviet Union a scant 21 years later. Finally it was reborn as a Communist state under Soviet control after World War II.

[1]Excerpt from an article by William E. Schaufele, Jr., U.S. Ambassador to Poland from June to September 1980 and a career diplomat. *Headline Series.* 256:8–34. O. '81. Copyright © 1981 by The Foreign Policy Association, Inc. Reprinted by permission.

The birth of Poland generally dates from 966 A.D. when King Mieszko I, through his marriage to a Bohemian princess, was baptized as a Roman Catholic and spread Christianity throughout his lands, unifying the country under one religion. Ever since then the fate of the nation and the Church have been closely linked. During the next 1,000 years the fortunes of the Polish people waxed and waned.

After an initial period of integration and unification, the kingdom went into eclipse when Boleslaw III, before his death in 1138, divided Poland among his four sons, appointing one to act as "senior." In the process of vying for supremacy, the sons and their heirs dismembered the country, and so it remained for two centuries. The process of disintegration was checked by the unifying resistance to the Mongol invasion (1241–42), but it was not until the reign of Casimir III the Great in the early 14th century that most of Poland was reunified. The constitutional, administrative, economic and educational reforms which Casimir instituted made Poland an important European power. It was during Casimir's reign that Poland gave asylum to large numbers of Jews fleeing Germany; they were to become the backbone of Polish commerce, an activity which the Polish landed gentry disdained.

The accession of the Jagiellonian dynasty in 1382 marked the beginning of four centuries of consolidation and expansion in which Polish culture and influence flowered. Poland was united with Lithuania in 1386, making the country four times as large as the original kingdom and over twice as large as present-day Poland. The first three Jagiellonian kings consolidated the union by breaking the power of the Teutonic Knights in Pomerania and along the Baltic coast. They established the border only 90 miles west of Moscow. And they annexed Bohemia and parts of modern-day Hungary. Internally, the power of the nobility grew and a form of parliamentarianism was established.

The period of 1492–1572, often characterized as Poland's Golden Age, was not a peaceful one. Invading Turks, Tatars and Muscovites threatened the outlying areas of the Polish empire— present-day Ukraine, Belorussia, Lithuania and Rumania. Poland not only survived all of these conflicts, but it simultaneously made progress toward unifying what was then known as a commonwealth.

The full unification of Poland and Lithuania was achieved in 1569 with the creation of a two-chamber parliament and one of the earliest constitutional monarchies, interestingly enough known as a Royal Republic. Domestic and foreign trade boomed and spirited intellectual activity flourished. The second university in Central and Eastern Europe had been established in Krakow in 1364. It was there, during the Golden Age, that Nicolaus Copernicus first studied astronomy, which eventually led to his revolutionary planetary theory. It has been estimated that 25 percent of the Polish population could read and write by 1580, an astonishing proportion compared to the rest of the world.

The Golden Age was followed by the Silver Age (1572–1648). In a brief interregnum, the principle of an elected monarch was institutionalized, thus increasing the power of the nobles at the king's expense. Eventually the power of the nobility was concentrated in handful of landed families who could organize or "buy" the support of the less affluent nobles—the beginning of the end of effective political organization. The parliament (*Sejm*) in the mid-16th century adopted the *liberum veto* system, that is, legislation had to be passed unanimously, which meant it could be blocked by the objection of any single member. This frequently brought the business of government to a complete standstill.

It was during the Silver Age that Poland became known as the "granary of Europe" and enjoyed an economic boom. Farm estates were enlarged, the land was exploited and so, too, was peasant labor. Poland's image as a granary has endured. Even though modern Poland is less than half its former size and no longer occupies the rich lands it did 400 years ago, some Poles and foreigners alike still think of it as a rich agricultural country, forced to sell its excess production to the Soviet Union. Actually, Polish land, with few exceptions, is poor in quality, and the country has not been self-sufficient in agriculture since it lost the eastern lands in 1945.

After 1648 Poland was frequently a battlefield where Poles fought Cossacks, Tatars and Russians, Swedes and Turks. Perhaps more important for modern Polish history, Poland's territory became a pawn in the fierce competition between Russia and Prussia. Peter the Great, in blocking King Frederick William I's effort to annex land the Prussian claimed, gained control of the

Baltic seacoast in 1716. Frederick II the Great later annexed Silesia. And Poland was the stage for major battles between Prussia and Russia during the Seven Years' War (1756–63).

Partition: Eclipse of the Polish State

The increasing weakness of the Polish regime combined with the incessant conflicts between Prussia, Russia and Austria—all of which used Poland to launch attacks on their adversaries and as a potential source of additional land and resources—led to the First Partition of Poland. For all practical purposes, the partition by Prussia, Russia and Austria in 1772 ended Poland's existence as an independent state for a century and a half—until 1918.

The First Partition deprived Poland of 28 percent of its territory. This so shocked Polish leaders that they enacted a series of reforms, including abolition of the liberum veto and other obstructions to effective government. The reforms culminated in the Constitution of May 3, 1791, which established the concepts of "people's sovereignty"; the separation of powers among the executive, legislative and judiciary; and the responsibility of the cabinet to parliament. It was the first written constitution since the U.S. Constitution of 1789, and the anniversary of its adoption is still celebrated by people of Polish origin all over the world.

The reforms were considered so dangerous by Russia that it invaded Poland in 1792. This led to the Second Partition, which involved only Prussia and Russia.

The Second Partition in turn precipitated a Polish revolt in 1794 led by Tadeusz Kosciuszko, who had fought with distinction in the American Revolutionary War. Despite some initial successes the revolt was eventually crushed, and the remainder of Poland was subjected to a third and complete partition in 1795.

Although Poland had suffered many vicissitudes during the preceding eight centuries, the next 123 years of Polish history played a large, almost determining role in forming modern Polish attitudes toward many issues. The partition of Poland among three foreign powers snuffed out the existence of a Polish state but, at the same time, it strengthened and intensified the feeling of Polish nationhood and nationalism.

Not that the situation within Poland remained static—far from it. Initially, for instance, the Polish Constitution, culture and administration remained relatively unaffected in the Russian sector, in part because Russia simply lacked qualified administrators. In the other two sectors, however, Polish officials were usually replaced by Prussians and Austrians.

In 1807 Napoleon Bonaparte established the semi-autonomous Duchy of Warsaw after he defeated the Prussians. However, after his advance on Moscow in 1812 failed, the Duchy fell under Russian rule. The Congress of Vienna (1814–15), which redrew the map of Europe after Napoleon's downfall, eventually created a Kingdom of Poland (or Congress Poland as it came to be called) within the Russian empire. Although Congress Poland had its own Constitution, parliament and army, the Russian czar ruled harshly, without regard for the provisions of the Congress of Vienna. In 1830 and again in 1863 the Poles rebelled unsuccessfully against Russian rule; they rose against Prussia in 1846. After 1864 the control of the three partitioning powers, in differing ways, was total.

The Russian sector of Poland was gradually "Russified" over the years. Schooling was in Russian and the institutions of higher education became Russian. Similarly, in the Prussian sector of Poland, German became the language of instruction. The Prussians, however, did develop the economy and therefore the skills of Polish workers in the area. Only in the Austrian sector of Poland did Polish remain the teaching language. And indeed the Poles were represented in the Austrian parliament as the "second" nationality in the multinational Hapsburg Empire. This period also was marked by massive emigration, mostly from southern Poland to the United States. Other large Polish émigré groups, including a great proportion of the politically active aristocracy and intelligentsia, lived in France and Germany.

During this whole partition period, Poles who remained in the homeland organized themselves into secret societies or, later, into political parties with the aim of reconstituting an independent Poland. Some groups engaged in revolutionary violence while others pursued a more evolutionary policy.

The three main political parties of post-World War I Poland were in fact established during the partition period, although not all of them were allowed to operate openly in Poland. National Democracy (ND) under the leadership of Roman Dmowski emerged in 1905 but had its roots in earlier political groups dating back to 1886. Since it initially advocated only Polish autonomy, it was allowed to function in the Russian sector. The Polish Socialist party (PPS) was founded in 1892. Operating clandestinely, it split in 1905–6 into a nationalist wing, led by Jozef Pilsudski, and an internationalist wing, which eventually merged with Rosa Luxemburg's small Communist organization, the Social Democracy of the Kingdom of Poland and Lithuania. The third major party, the Polish Peasant party (PSL), came into being in 1907 in the Austrian sector and participated in Austrian politics. No Polish political grouping was tolerated in the German sector, which had been fully integrated into Bismark's Reich in the late 19th century.

Independence, 1918–39

Poland once more became a battlefield during World War I, but Polish patriots saw a possibility of exploiting the conflict to regain Polish independence. Dmowski and his group formed the Polish National Committee in Paris in 1914 and supported the Russian war effort. Pilsudski, however, formed the Polish Legions which fought with the Austrian forces against Russia. Pilsudski eventually became disillusioned with the Central Powers when he realized they opposed a fully independent Poland and that independence could only be achieved through an Allied victory, followed by the gradual collapse and disintegration of the three partitioning powers. He and many of his supporters were eventually interned in Germany.

The success of the Russian Revolution in 1917, which both Dmowski and Pilsudski opposed, helped bring their groups together. Dmowski was not interested in associating with a Communist Russia and thereafter cooperated with the Western Allies. Pilsudski was well-known for his hatred of Russia, Czarist and Bolshevik alike. The fact that President Woodrow Wilson had made independence for Poland the thirteenth of his famous Fourteen Points was an added reason for cooperating with the Allies.

Although the two men worked together in 1918, with Dmowski as head of the Polish delegation to the Versailles Conference and Pilsudski as acting chief of state and army commander in the newly created independent Poland, Pilsudski was the dominant force during the period 1919–39. Even though he died in 1935, his political heirs dominated Polish politics for the next four years, until the Nazi invasion.

The re-creation of an independent Poland in 1918 was followed by a series of events which sowed the seeds of later instability and unrest in Central Europe:

• the creation of a Polish Corridor to the sea, with the port of Danzig (now Gdansk) as a "free city" under the administration of the League of Nations, which became the basis of future claims against Poland by both the Weimar Republic and Nazi Germany;

• the holding of plebiscites in the regions of Silesia and Masuria to determine whether they were to be joined to Poland or Germany, with results that were unsatisfactory to both parties;

• the division of the area of Cieszyn in Silesia between Poland and Czechoslovakia, leaving a Polish enclave inside the latter; and, finally,

• the creation of more than 80 political parties, a reflection of the Polish zest for pluralism. Some were ethnic, but many were composed of both Poles and ethnic groups, which splintered from other parties. Poland's population was heterogeneous: only 65 percent were ethnically Polish; the rest belonged to minority groups (Ukrainians, White Russians, Germans, Jews), many of them hostile to each other and to the Poles.

As the Soviet Union, following the defeat of Germany and the uncertainty over the new Polish republic's boundaries, advanced its western border from the Dnieper to the Bug rivers between 1918 and 1919, the infant state of Poland quickly organized an army which drove the Soviet forces all the way to Kiev and recaptured territory in the north, including Wilno. The Soviets, as internal resistance to the Lenin regime crumbled, counterattacked and by August 1920 were at the gates of Warsaw. But Pilsudski, despite his lack of formal military training, perceiving a weakness in the Soviet front, counterattacked and drove the Red Army east. The Treaty of Riga, signed in 1921, restored the Polish eastern boundary on the Dnieper and again gave Poland Wilno and Lvov, both important commercial and intellectual centers in Polish history.

Internally, although preserving democratic forms, Pilsudski ruled as an autocrat supported by the army, led primarily by his former officers of the Polish Legions. After 1922 he formerly "retired" from politics but continued to exert great influence. Concerned with the direction and insufficiencies of the regime, in 1926 he rallied his former Legion commanders and overthrew the government. Although he refused the Polish presidency and would take no official position except that of minister of defense, Pilsudski in fact ruled Poland.

Whatever the popular affection Pulsudski enjoyed, he was never able to form a democratically elected government. The ND and the Peasant party were the most powerful political groups. When he did form a nonparty bloc to overcome parliamentary hindrances to his policies, he was still unable to win the majority needed to amend the Constitution as he wished to do.

Pilsudski and his supporters tried to follow an independent foreign policy, consistent with the longstanding Polish hope of avoiding being a pawn, a battleground or a dependency of either Germany or Russia—or the Soviet Union. Traditionally there have been two schools of thought in Polish foreign policy: the romantic, which asserted Poland's independent role; and the realistic, which believed that Poland must inevitably become associated with either Germany or Russia for its own protection. As Dmowski once phrased it: "Either Russia or Germany but never both."

The new republic under Pilsudski reflected the romantic tradition; it even expected that by pursuing a policy of independence it could become an important European power. The policy was based on a gross underestimation of German and Russian hostility to Poland's existence and their desire to reverse the provisions of the Versailles and Riga treaties. Much as Pilsudski hated the Russians, he had no intention of allying Poland with Germany. Instead, Poland concluded nonaggression agreements with both the Soviet Union and Germany. In 1921 it had allied itself with

France and, early in 1939, with Britain. Psychologically, Poland took comfort in those alliances, and it ignored what was obvious to any objective observer—that in the event of attack neither France nor Britain could provide immediate assistance.

Poland was further weakened by Pilsudski's and others' failures to modernize the Polish armed forces. Few armies have the élan and esprit of the Polish army, but esprit was not enough when the equipment and organization of the defense forces remained hopelessly out of date.

In retrospect, Poland, from 1919 to 1939, had boundless problems. Militarily, its armed forces were unprepared and unequipped for modern warfare. Economically, the country's development suffered from neglect. Tension with both the Soviet Union and Germany was almost constant—relieved only occasionally by short-term considerations of Central European politics, which forced one or both to concentrate their attentions elsewhere. Internal tension was exacerbated by the failure, despite relative freedom of speech, to achieve even nominally democratic rule in the face of a determined autocrat like Pilsudski. There was continuous friction among the various nationalities in Poland, exemplified during World War II by the reported atrocities carried out by the Ukrainians and Lithuanians recruited by the Nazis. The attempt to play a skillful and clever game between the Soviets and the Germans failed. And at least as long as the World War I Allies were unwilling to make their weight felt, there was no way to forestall German demands for the return of the Polish Corridor and Danzig. On September 1, 1939, Poland became the first World War II victim of the Nazi blitzkrieg, and was again partitioned when the Soviet Union invaded from the east on September 17. Independent Poland disappeared for six more years.

Communist Poland

Poland emerged from World War II as perhaps the most deeply scarred country with the exception of Germany itself. Initially occupied by both Nazi Germany and the U.S.S.R., it had later been totally occupied by Germany. Subsequently, when Soviet forces had driven the German army westward, Poland once again had become a battlefield for the two large powers and, at least for a time, had been subjected to Soviet occupation.

The physical devastation was vast. Warsaw itself, as a result of war damage and a deliberate German effort to level it, suffered up to 85 percent destruction, according to some observers. More important, Poland lost 6 million people, or about 17 percent of its prewar population. Over half of those who died were Jews, who numbered 3.5 million in 1939. Only 625,000 people were killed as a result of military activity. The rest were executed in concentration camps, killed in city or ghetto reprisals, or died as a result of conditions in the camps or the generally poor living conditions in wartime Poland. The population of Poland was further depleted as a result of postwar exchanges of territory and forced or voluntary repatriation. The population immediately after the war was estimated at 23.6 million, down from 34.8 million in 1939.

The whole of Poland was pushed geographically westward some 125 to 150 miles as a result of boundary changes after the war. The eastern area lost to the Soviet Union exceeded the gain represented by the German territory east of the Oder-Neisse river line. Many Poles still have a strong attachment to the eastern lands even though most of those who lived there chose to be resettled in present-day Poland.

Polish politics did not take a wartime holiday. Many Polish political leaders fled Poland in 1939 and established a government-in-exile, first in France and, after 1940, in London. Many of the leaders of the small Polish Communist party, which had been dissolved by the Communist International, or Comintern, in 1938, fled to the Soviet Union.

Resistance groups were organized in Poland almost immediately after the German and Soviet occupations. The largest was the Home Army (AK), directed by the government-in-exile. The Soviet Union had annexed the areas it occupied and deported large numbers of Poles to the Soviet interior, many to slave labor camps. After the Nazi attack on the U.S.S.R. in 1941, the government-in-exile made its peace with Moscow. Poles in the U.S.S.R. enlisted in Polish units, organized and trained by the Soviet army, and they were commanded by Polish General Wladyslaw Anders. When the Soviets, over the objections of the Western Allies and the Polish military leaders, insisted on committing the Polish forces to battle in separate units rather than as a national force, most of the Polish units departed the Soviet Union. Under General Anders, 230,000 fought with distinction in North Africa, Italy and Western Europe. Moscow subsequently recruited a force from among the Poles who remained in the Soviet Union. They were commanded largely by Soviet officers since most of the surviving prewar Polish officer corps had left with Anders or had escaped to the West.

Well after the Home Army was founded, a second resistance group known as the People's Army (AL) was organized by the Polish Worker's party (PPR). The PPR was the official name of the Polish Communist party, which the Soviet Union reconstituted in 1942.

Relations between the Soviet Union and the London government-in-exile became increasingly strained as the U.S.S.R. reiterated its determination to retain the eastern territories after the war. Relations were finally severed over the question of responsibility for the Katyn Forest massacre. In 1943 the Germans announced the discovery of mass graves of over 10,000 Polish officers executed by Soviet authorities in the Katyn Forest near Smolensk in 1940. The Polish authorities in London insisted on an investigation by the International Red Cross. The Soviets claimed the executions were the work of the Germans and used this demand as a pretext to break relations. The German version has been generally accepted in the West by objective observers.

Thereafter there were essentially two Polish political groups: the London government-in-exile, a coalition of prewar Polish party leaders, directing the Home Army, which claimed a strength of 380,000 men and women; and the PPR, directed from Moscow, whose People's Army operated in conjunction with the Red Army.

Warsaw Uprising

The most concentrated resistance to the German occupation took place in the capital. In 1943 Warsaw's Jewish population rose against the Germans in a desperate and heroic struggle doomed to failure. A number of factors combined to drive the Jews into open rebellion. They had been pressed into a smaller and smaller ghetto; they were forced to select people for deportation and labor details; they realized that Jews were actually being exterminated; and they were receiving fewer and fewer services and goods, including food. However, general knowledge of the "Final Solution," the elimination of all Jews, was not yet widespread or simply was not believed.

More significant perhaps, in terms of Poland's future, was the Warsaw uprising of 1944. It began on August 1 and lasted for 63 days. Some aspects of this event, which captured the attention of the world, are subject to dispute. According to one version, as Soviet troops moved closer to Warsaw, Radio Moscow called upon the citizens of Warsaw to rise against the German occupation. However, the Soviet offensive stopped on the outskirts of the city, and the Red Army stood by as the Home Army was defeated and the city of Warsaw was systematically destroyed by the occupying Germans. According to this version, Moscow deliberately provoked the annihilation of the largest and most effective Polish resistance group, which also happened to be anti-Communist, in order to destroy a potentially effective postwar opposition to Soviet domination. A variation of this version is that, although the Soviet forces had indeed reached the outskirts of Warsaw, they were forced to retreat by German counterattacks on their exposed salient, which had advanced ahead of the rest of the Soviet forces. The fact that the Soviets refused landing rights to Allied aircraft, which could have dropped food and supplies to the Polish resistance in Warsaw but needed to refuel in the Soviet Union, tends to support the arguments of those who believe the Soviets deliberately sought the defeat of the Home Army.

Another version, however, maintains that the London government-in-exile wished the Home Army to liberate Warsaw before the Soviets arrived in order to strengthen and reinforce its claim to legitimacy as the postwar ruler of Poland. If true, the decision to launch the uprising may have been precipitated ten days earlier by the Soviet-supported establishment of the Polish Committee of National Liberation (PKWN)—generally known as the Lublin Committee—in Chelm. The Lublin Committee posed a direct threat to the hopes of the London government-in-exile.

Whatever one's view of this historic event, the result was the destruction of the military arm of the government-in-exile and a significant boost to the aspirations of the Polish Communist leaders. Their quest for power was further encouraged by the Western Allies' inability or unwillingness successfully to challenge the Soviet claim to the eastern territory annexed in 1939. However, the history of postwar Poland would probably have been no different in any case, since Soviet troops effectively occupied the country. The U.S.S.R. certainly would not have permitted Poland to strike out on an independent, probably pro-Western course which could have threatened Soviet hegemony in Eastern Europe.

With Poland's eastern boundary settled by Soviet fiat in January 1945, there remained the question of the western boundary. The Soviets and the Poles demanded the so-called Oder-Neisse line, approximately 150 miles west of the prewar boundary. The Allies strongly resisted this demand at the Potsdam Conference in 1945, but they acquiesced in and actually facilitated the resettlement of the German population from the area. The Allies accepted the Oder-Neisse line, first as a temporary boundary but later, in the absence of a permanent peace treaty—as of 1981 still to be accomplished—as the de facto final frontier.

The Soviet Union did agree to Western demands for a coalition government in Poland—but it was a coalition more in name than substance. Organs of the Lublin Committee had already been transformed into a provisional government and parliament, and the People's Army had been integrated into the First Polish Army, which then became the Polish People's Army. Nevertheless Stanislaw Mikolajczyk, the prewar Polish Peasant party leader who had been prime minister of the government-in-exile, returned to Warsaw in July 1945 to become a deputy prime minister along with PPR leader Wladyslaw Gomulka in a Provisional Government of 20 cabinet members, 17 of them from the Lublin Committee.

Making of a Satellite

During the next 18 months the Polish Communists consolidated their position in what has become the classical Communist formula. With the daunting help of the Soviet Union, they created trade unions, mass organizations and front groups, and infiltrated existing groups. The establishment of Polish national authority over territory gained from Germany and the resettlement of the population from the land lost to the Soviet Union provided special opportunities to manipulate circumstances to their own advantage. Even Mikolajczyk had to organize a new Polish Peasant party when the old one was successfully infiltrated.

Parliamentary elections were held in January 1947. The Communist PPR and four other parties presented a single list of candidates while the new Peasant party offered an independent list—the only party permitted to do so. The elections were rigged in favor of the Communists and their allies; intimidation and terror were commonplace; only the Communist-led list of candidates had access to the media; Peasant party meetings were broken up, its candidates often arrested; and the police prevented voters from casting their ballots in secret. The results were unsurprising: 417 seats to the Communist-led list, 27 to the opposition. Thus the Communists legitimized their regime by an election victory they had used any and all means to obtain.

The monopoly of power in the hands of the Polish Communists and their Soviet backers had not prevented the formation of an anti-Communist resistance as early as September 1945. It took the Communist party, using the organs of the government, the militia and the army, two years to quell that resistance. Casualties were heavy. Gomulka himself later wrote that over 20,000 Communists and several thousand militia and army personnel had been killed. There are no confirmed figures of deaths among the anti-Communist resistance.

Full consolidation of power took the Communists somewhat longer. After the 1947 elections a new government was formed with Boleslaw Beirut, later first secretary of the PPR, as president and Jozef Cyrankiewicz, a leader of the Polish Socialist party, as prime minister. Gomulka remained as a vice prime minister, but Mikolajczyk was dropped and a few months later fled Poland. In 1948 the Polish Socialist party and the Communist Polish Workers' party were merged and renamed the Polish United Workers' party (PZPR). A United Peasant party (ZSL) and a Democratic party (SD) favorable to the Communist regime were also formed.

One of the final steps in the consolidation of Communist power in Poland was the purge of Gomulka in 1948. Gomulka, significantly, had been the secretary-general of the PPR at its founding in German-occupied Poland and thus automatically was the political head of the Communist People' s Army. Unlike many of the other party leaders he did not spend the war years in Moscow. As Stalin moved to create a monolithic Eastern Europe, including the formation of the Communist Information Bureau, or Cominform, in 1947, Gomulka objected. He had also supported a moderate stance toward Tito's Yugoslavia. Moscow categorized Gomulka as a "rightist-nationalist" deviationist and removed him from all of his posts. He was actually incarcerated for three years.

The Cow Is Saddled

By the end of 1948 Poland was firmly in the hands of the Communist regime and under Soviet control. There remained only one more move to complete the political transformation: the formation of the National Unity Front in 1951, which included the PZPR, the United Peasant party and the Democratic party as well as the mass organizations. The Polish Communists controlled and manipulated the National Unity Front for their own purposes.

Like most of its Eastern European neighbors, Poland was forced to adopt the Soviet system and follow the Soviet model in structuring the government and party which ruled Communist Poland—this despite the fact that Stalin allegedly once remarked that the imposition of communism in Poland was like trying to saddle a cow.

The years 1948–56 probably represented the nadir of Communist Poland; the "Sovietization" of the country was never more pronounced than during this period. With the cold war increasingly dominating international affairs, the Soviet Union demanded orthodoxy and subservience from its allies in Eastern Europe. The term "Soviet satellite" had real and accurate meaning. Not only was Poland denied the right to make independent decisions, even on internal matters, but it also suffered the ultimate indignity of having a Soviet marshal, Konstantin Rokossovsky, as minister of defense and commander in chief of the Polish People's Army. Soviet officers held other high positions in the Polish armed forces, and Soviet officials held top posts in the government, particularly in the security services.

The death of Stalin in 1953 did not produce any immediate relief, though Moscow did begin to relax its grip—none too rapidly, however, in the case of Poland. Soviet-Yugoslav rapprochement in 1955 and the dismantling of the Cominform in 1956 contributed to the general easing of Stalinist control over Eastern Europe. And in Poland, writers and academic figures began to publish critiques on the Polish political situation which inevitably pointed toward the "Polish road to socialism."

Poznan Riots

The death of the PZPR First Secretary Bierut in 1956 necessitated a change in Polish leadership. Bierut was replaced in March by Edward Ochab, but Gomulka, who had been released from prison in 1954 after three years without trial, was lingering in the wings waiting to be rehabilitated.

Then, in June 1956, Polish workers engaged in their first action which led to the fall of a Polish Communist leadership. Workers in Poznan rioted for better living conditions and greater economic and political freedom. Local internal security forces were unable to control the situation, and the army refused to fire on Polish workers. Finally an elite internal security brigade from Warsaw suppressed the rioting but with such brutality that even greater dissension spread throughout the country.

As public discontent grew, the PZPR leadership was under increasing pressure not only to change economic policies, which it had begun to do in a tentative way, but to change the leadership as well. This pressure coincided with the readmission of Gomulka to party membership in August 1956.

Why did Gomulka, who had been the first Communist party leader in Poland after the war and had led Poland not only into communism but also into the Soviet camp, become the beneficiary of popular support? Gomulka was the people's and the party's choice in a state dominated by one party because he was perceived as a Pole first and a Communist second; because he appeared to promise a better life and a more open society; and because he might reduce Soviet influence. Thus, eight years after his ouster at the behest of the Soviet Union, the rightist-nationalist deviation of which he was then accused had become the very reason for his political popularity. He was seen as someone who had defied the Soviet Union, had courageously defended himself, and was above all a Polish nationalist.

The Soviet Union, however, was less than enthusiastic about the prospect of a Gomulka regime and the internal liberalization that would probably accompany it. Communist party Chairman Nikita S. Khrushchev led an uninvited and unexpected Soviet delegation on a visit to Warsaw in October 1956 just as it became apparent that Gomulka, only three months after being readmitted to the party, was about to become first secretary of the Communist party once again. At the same time, Soviet troops stationed in Poland started to move toward the capital. Polish troops loyal to Gomulka responded by taking up defensive positions around Warsaw.

Discussions between the two party leaderships were described in a Polish commentary as "temperamental," but there was no armed clash as there would be in Hungary. Soviet troops were recalled to their garrisons, Khrushchev returned to Moscow apparently satisfied that the "Polish October" would not go beyond permissible limits, and Gomulka was formally named first secretary. To what extent the mounting crisis in Hungary—which exploded only three days later—may have affected the Soviet decision is unknown.

Khrushchev, in his memoirs, is relatively candid about the situation at that time. He claims that Gomulka told the Soviet delegation that, if Soviet troops were not stopped, "something terrible and irreversible will happen." Khrushchev added, "As we began to calculate which Polish regiments we could count on, the situation began to look somewhat bleak"—this despite the dominant position of Soviet officers among the armed forces. Khrushchev concluded, "It would have been a fatal conflict with grave consequences that would have been felt for many years."

Polish Winter, Czech Spring

Rokossovsky and other Soviet officers and most of the Soviet technical advisers to the Polish regime returned to the Soviet Union. A "status of forces" agreement which gave the Poles some control over the Soviet forces in Poland was concluded. And the Polish army, which had lost the trust of the people, began rebuilding itself as a Polish institution to regain its traditional respect and popularity as a profession. However, Gomulka's apparent victory in gaining grudging Soviet acquiescence to the "Polish road to socialism" had definite limitations. It did not extend to any weakening of the bonds to the Soviet Union. Poland remained a member of the Warsaw Pact, the Soviet-Eastern European counterpart to the North Atlantic Treaty Organization (NATO), and of the Council for Mutual Economic Assistance (CMEA, also known as Comecon), and its foreign policy continued to bear Moscow's stamp. In fact, after his resumption of power in October 1956, Gomulka supported Soviet intervention in Hungary, even though Polish public opinion strongly supported the Hungarian "freedom fighters," a fact which Radio Warsaw admitted at one point. Twelve years later, Polish troops participated in the overthrow of Alexander Dubcek's regime in Czechoslovakia.

Many of the encouraging acts and policies which accompanied Gomulka's resumption of power were modified or reversed as time went on. Gomulka had earlier emphasized the bilateral aspects of relations between the members of the Warsaw Pact while Moscow stressed their multilateral dimension. Poland's relations with Yugoslavia, for instance, were always somewhat closer than Moscow's. Yet gradually Poland fitted its relations within and outside the Communist world more and more into a Soviet mold. In spite of warnings from the Soviet Union, Gomulka had initially reached out to the West (the United States provided $52.9 million in Public Law 480 food assistance between 1957–63), but he subsequently took a hard public line toward the United States.

Internally the hopes for economic reform, such as decentralization of planning and production and a more prominent role for the Yugoslav-like workers' councils established in 1956, gradually diminished. Gomulka did successfully resist Soviet pressure to pursue the collectivization of agriculture. However, relations with the Church, which had recommenced on such a hopeful note in 1956 with the release of the primate, Stefan Cardinal Wyszynski, after three years' imprisonment, waxed and waned over the 14 years Gomulka was in power. The irresistible tendency of Polish intellectuals to speak out caused recurring difficulties for Gomulka during this period. The encouraging developments of 1956 never did blossom fully again.

The factionalism within the PZPR, which surfaced in the struggle preceding Gomulka's return, did not ease during this entire period. One group consisted of traditional Communists while the other tended to be Communist with a strong tinge of nationalism. Such an internal tug-of-war is not unusual, even in a totalitarian society, and it may in part account for Gomulka's seeming inconsistency in moving from one side of an issue to another, apparently in an effort to placate both factions.

From 1964 on, led by General Mieczyslaw Moczar, minister of interior, the "partisans," a group within the party which had remained in Poland during the war and espoused a kind of national but hardline communism, seemed to gain increasing strength within the party. Their influence on policy provoked student opposition—especially at Warsaw University—in 1968 and a wave of anti-Semitism which resulted in the expulsion or voluntary departure of many of the few remaining Jews in Poland. There is reason to believe that anti-Semitism was used as a weapon in the internal party struggle. Because some Stalinist party leaders had been Jews, this group equated Jewishness with Stalinism. Communist and non-Communist alike, the Jewish community felt the effects. After 1968 Gomulka's fortunes went steadily downhill.

In 1956 Gomulka had been the people's choice, but his policies over 12 years had become increasingly repressive; living did not become much easier for the Polish population; and, although the Soviets did not have the ubiquitous role they had had earlier, the people tended to blame many of Gomulka's policies and actions on Soviet influence. And certainly the "Polish road to socialism" had never been completed.

Enter Gierek

Gomulka's last important act was the signing in 1970 of a treaty with the Federal Republic of Germany, which recognized the Polish postwar western border and opened up diplomatic and commercial relations between the two countries. It was an historic moment when Willy Brandt, the West German chancellor, knelt before the monument erected to the heroes of the Warsaw uprising and in effect, ended the state of war between Poland and Germany.

But it was not enough to save Gomulka. His downfall was precipitated by another outbreak of labor violence that year. Long-simmering public discontent over the shortages of basic foodstuffs and housing, dependence on the Soviet Union, and the lack of freedom exploded, as it was to do later, over the announcement of widespread price increases. Anti-regime feeling took its most violent form in Gdansk, where shipyard workers took to the streets and burned the party headquarters. The result was an estimated 70 workers killed by the internal security forces. Gomulka was deposed and replaced as first secretary by Edward Gierek, a member of the Politburo and the party chief in Silesia.

Not as popular as Gomulka when he resumed power, Gierek was nevertheless respected for what he, a former miner, had been able to achieve in improving conditions in Silesia. He had not spent the war years in Poland, but neither had he spent them in the Soviet Union. He had worked as a miner in both France and Belgium and in fact had become a Communist in France.

He promised change, and to a certain extent he accomplished it—at least for a while. Essentially the new leader's policies consisted of four major elements: increases in real wages; better supplies of consumer goods; stable prices for basic necessities; and modernization, *i.e.* industrialization, of the economy. Foreign credits were available, imported goods helped to fill the gaps in Polish production, real wage increases and increased supplies of consumer goods were incentives to increased productivity, agricultural production was rising, and the global economy was reasonably healthy. The psychological atmosphere caused by a change in the regime and the concessions to consumerism led to rising expectations and hope for the future. New goals obviously could not be realized immediately, but economic activity gradually increased. For the mass of the Polish people life did improve . . .

To finance the modernization program, Poland turned to the West, incurring large debts to Western governments and banks. Many licensing agreements were made with Western firms— Grundig radios, International Harvester tractors, Fiat automobile, and others. Other contracts were let for whole plants—RCA and Corning Glass collaborated on the construction of one of the most modern TV color-picture tube plants in the world, in part thanks to credits from the U.S. Export-Import Bank. Other loans were made for chemical, machinery, machine tool, motor vehicle, food processing, plastics, tobacco, soft drinks, tourist and other industries.

The assumption was that once completed many of these industries would be producing for export, which would earn the hard currency to repay the loans. However, several factors operated to nullify this hope:

• The recession in the West in 1974–75, following the Arab oil boycott, reduced the market for Polish goods.

• Polish production, although probably of higher quality than that of many Communist countries, often failed to meet Western standards.

• Polish reach exceeded its grasp: the timely completion of construction projects and the meeting of production quotas depended on greater efficiency than the Poles could achieve.

• The regime paid little attention to marketing skills and techniques but depended on its Western partners to provide them; obviously the partners were less interested in selling Polish products than their own.

• There was inadequate flexibility and incentive for the export industries.

• As the foreign debt grew, more emphasis was placed on new credits to pay interest and principal than on improved and more productive industry.

Although most experts recognized and acknowledged many of the above problems, the leadership did not have enough courage even to begin the necessary reforms. Moreover, the commitment to maintain stable prices required increasing subsidies which eventually consumed one-third of the budget. The availability of consumer goods gradually declined. Poles were spending more and more time in lines to purchase the most necessary staples, such as meat and butter, and this reduced even further the productivity of the economy. And as spending power increased so did demand, which could not be met.

Agricultural productivity did not increase. Partly this was due to adverse weather conditions in the years 1974–80. But earlier efforts to induce collectivization had made the peasants, traditionally suspicious of the state, even more wary than usual. At those times when the regime seemed to hold out incentives, the peasants tended to believe that this was a temporary palliative and not to be trusted. Furthermore, resources necessary for increased production—fertilizer, seed, spare parts—were diverted to the inefficient state agricultural sector. Therefore the private farmers had neither the incentives nor the means to increase production significantly. The emphasis on industrialization meant that many peasants switched to wage-earning jobs and produced only enough agricultural goods for their own needs.

Eventually the regime lost its ability to communicate with the people who, more and more, regarded everything the regime said with increasing skepticism and outright disbelief. The statements of the national leadership, dutifully repeated by the local officials, were so obviously in contradiction to life as the people knew it that the latter intended to disregard the statements entirely. The earlier promise of "dialogue" proved false, and local officials could not or would not communicate the real social and economic problems of the people to the leadership.

60 DAYS THAT SHOOK POLAND[2]

The euphoria has evaporated. The inspiring belief that the 60-day workers' revolt which shook Poland to its foundations this summer might cleanse and transform what had for 35 years been a dreary national existence has been tempered recently by the sober realization that change does not come that easily. There is a sense that events are spinning out of control and heading for disaster. Many Poles feel they are living on borrowed time.

The slogan of *odnowa,* which means "rebirth," is still heard, but now it sounds more like a plea than a promise. In homes, as in Government ministries, the talk is not so much about workers' rights and reconstruction as about more strikes, confrontation and Soviet tanks.

It is a far cry from the hope and optimism of Aug. 31, when the all-powerful Communist state, in the person of Mieczyslaw Jagielski, a well-tailored, slightly bald First Deputy Prime Minister, who found the glare of the television lights disquieting because they reminded him of his years inside a Nazi concentration camp, sat down to sign the agreement that ended the Baltic coast strikes with Lech Walesa, an unemployed electrician with a Pancho Villa mustache, who had scrambled over the wall of the Lenin Shipyard to lead a workers' insurrection that brought the Government to its knees.

The strike, the Gdansk agreement, the two months of labor turmoil that preceded it and everything that has happened since, are the most significant events in Eastern Europe since Yugoslavia was expelled from the Soviet bloc in 1948. As Tito broke the myth of monolithic Communism with a "separate road to socialism," the Gdansk strikers have broken the myth—in Poland, at least—that the Communist Party speaks for the working class. The right to strike and to form independent trade unions could be as historic an advance for participatory socialism inside the Soviet bloc as the Magna Carta was for Western parliamentarianism.

[2]Reprint of an article by John Darnton, Bureau Chief of the *New York Times* in Warsaw. *New York Times Magazine.* p 39–41+. N. 9, '80. Copyright © 1980 by The New York Times Company. Reprinted by permission.

But everything depends upon what happens now, during an unsettling interregnum. So far, the signs are not good. The strikes unleashed years of pent-up frustrations and anger, and an earlier mood for reform has given way to calls for more radical changes. There is a touch of feistiness in the air.

Many of the independent unions that are springing up all over the country like mushrooms after a rain are making it abundantly clear they have no intention of knuckling under to the state, nor are they willing to compromise, even a bit, to help the Government convince its worried allies that Poland is not really slipping down the dark road of socialistic heresy.

Poland's neighbors, Czechoslovakia and East Germany, both "hard-line" countries, were quick to join the Soviet Union in openly condemning the "anti-Socialist elements" inside Poland, a line now being replaced by intensified Soviet charges of subversive attempts directed from the West. East Germany has gone on to abandon its policy of rapprochement with West Germany, imposing new currency regulations to discourage visits across the border, and then, in a stunning rebuke to a fellow Socialist country, has slapped down travel restrictions to and from Poland. A *cordon sanitaire* has been raised along all of Poland's borders.

There is, however, a slim chance that Poland will emerge relatively unscathed, if only because all of the principals in the ongoing drama—the Government, the workers and the Soviet Union—realize that any kind of outside intervention would have regrettable consequences.

Stanislaw Kania, who replaced Edward Gierek as the Polish United Workers' (Communist) Party boss after the strike was settled, has been conciliatory and moderate in his pronouncements, at least to date. But, other than that he is an apparatchik from deep inside the party's bosom, nothing much is known about him.

The Polish Government may well try to honor the Gdansk accord, in spirit as well as letter, allowing the new unions to assume an autonomous role as collective bargaining agents for the workers and opening up such institutions of national life as the press and universities to nonparty voices. If this occurs in a peaceful, evolutionary way, without significant outside interference, then Poland could become the first pluralistic society in the Communist world.

Unfortunately, other scenarios—all of them catastrophic—are equally likely: The new party leadership that came in with Kania, which really consists of old party faces in new positions, may try to renege on its pledge once the sense of crisis recedes, co-opting the unions, silencing the dissidents and halting the trend toward liberalization. The economy, already a shambles, may worsen even further so that discontent will erupt in new uprisings, this time coordinated and nationwide. The new unions could grow too big too fast and take on a political character that would threaten the party's "leading role" and engender a counterreaction.

Or the Soviet Union, deeply alarmed by the developments on its doorstep, may simply decide that enough is enough and send in its tanks. Such a move, many Western, Polish and some East European (other than Soviets, who don't talk) analysts feel, would trigger a full-scale Polish insurrection that would endanger world peace as much or more than the Berlin blockade, the Cuban missile crisis or the invasion of Afghanistan.

Poland, with its tradition of heroic but futile uprisings against Russian rule during the 123 years in which it was partitioned off the map, is continually suspect in the Kremlin. But Poland matters more to Moscow than any other country in the Soviet bloc. Its population, approaching 36 million, makes it bigger by far than any other Soviet satellite. It has the 12th largest gross national product in the world. It is homogeneous, headstrong and inclined to romanticism. And it has a history of rabid, anti-Russian nationalism.

Its stubborn and resilient peasantry has assiduously resisted collectivization; three-quarters of the farm land remains in private hands. Its fervent Catholicism, practiced by 90 percent of the people, has meant that the church has always been a competing institution to the ruling Communist Party, with a far deeper hold on the national psyche.

Except by a handful of theorists, socialism is not taken seriously as an ideology. It has an alien caste to it, a stigma of having been forcefully imposed from the outside. There is a broad conservative belt in Poland, encompassing everyone from peasants to students to middle-level bureaucrats, that looks to the West and fantasizes about what life would be like under capitalism.

The only Soviet satellite never to build a monument to Stalin, Poland was the first to throw off the stultifying cultural doctrine of socialist realism. And in 1956, it was the first satellite to de-Stalinize (liberalize), and workers' riots in Poznan brought Wladyslaw Gomulka to power against the wishes of Nikita S. Khrushchev, who ordered troops dispatched to Warsaw but changed his mind at the last moment. Moscow again contemplated intervention during the 1970 bread riots in Gdansk. But this time the Polish troops moved against the workers, and the violent suppression of the demonstrations later led to the toppling of Gomulka, who was replaced by Gierek.

After a temporary period of illusory prosperity, everything turned sour in the mid-1970's. Polish wage earners found that they had more money than ever before but few goods to spend it on. There was a stab at reform in 1976. But the general food price increase designed to reduce the burdensome system of subsidies was denounced by the workers, who rioted in Radom and Warsaw, burning down party headquarters and ripping up railroad tracks.

Gierek survived the next two years by striking an uneasy *modus vivendi* with the people; greater political tolerance to balance off the the growing economic misery. But the benefits of this policy were felt primarily by the intellectuals; the workers remained apathetic.

In 1979, two things happened to change that. Poland's national income—the closest equivalent to the West's gross national product—declined, for the first time since World War II. The only other Soviet satellite to have reached a negative growth level was Czechoslovakia—there it led to economic reforms that culminated in the ill-fated "Prague Spring" of 1968. Then there was the visit by Pope John Paul II, an event that unleashed a flood of national and religious pride and cut through the cocoon of anesthetized indifference that had surrounded the workers.

It is not surprising that the labor turmoil that rocked Poland last August should have exploded on the Baltic coast. There the sense of economic exploitation by the powerful neighbor to the east is markedly strong. The shipyards produce largely for a Soviet market, and the production is disadvantageous because Poland is required to equip the vessels with expensive equipment from the West, which must be paid for in hard currency.

The workers are rootless, volatile and prone to discontent, because they are first-generation proletarians who moved into the region to supplant the Germans in what had been Danzig and Stettin (now Gdansk and Szczecin). They are more given than most to anti-Soviet sentiment. Their fathers were peasants and laborers in the tiny villages and towns of the eastern territories gobbled up by Russia after the war.

They bitterly recall the brutal suppression of the 1970 demonstrations which caused hundreds of deaths. Many were politicized by that experience, which they refer to as a "war."

A handful of them began working with Poland's main dissident organization, the Committee for Social Self-Defense, known by its Polish acronym of KOR, which sprang up after the 1976 riots. KOR is the brainchild of Jacek Kuron, a former Communist who passed many of his frequent 48-hour detentions dreaming of forging an alliance for change between the intelligentsia and the workers.

Eleven months before the Baltic coast strikes, not many people noticed that KOR's *samizdat* newspaper, Robotnik (The Worker), had published a charter of workers' rights and a program for achieving them. Strikes, it said, are effective over the short run, but "in order not to waste the gains won," something more is required: free and independent trade unions. "Only they," the charter said, "can represent a power the authorities cannot ignore and will have to negotiate with on an equal footing." Among the 65 signatories to the document was Lech Walesa.

When Walesa climbed over the Lenin Shipyard wall on Aug. 14, the Gdansk strike was only a few hours old but Poland's labor turmoil had been going on for a month and a half, kicked off by surprise increases in meat prices on July 1.

What made the Gdansk strikers' action different was that instead of putting down their tools and walking off the job, they simply closed the shipyard gates and waited to see what would happen. What happened was that the Government floundered indecisively, the world press arrived, factories all across the country shut down in solidarity, and in no time at all the Gdansk strike leaders found themselves at the head of a burgeoning nationwide workers' revolt.

Walesa took a command role almost immediately because he was well known in the shipyard from preyious activism there, is charismatic and had the courage to assume a frontline position. He also had nothing to lose, since he didn't have a job there.

Two days after the Gdansk strike began it was effectively "settled." Walesa had negotiated a package that included a 12 percent wage increase. When he presented it, he was denounced for having sold out. "We walked off for you," shouted a bus driver. "How can our buses stand up to tanks alone?" A tactical leader who knows how to shift directions to keep up with the rank and file, Walesa abruptly declared the strike still on.

From that moment, the strikers were challenging not local, but state authorities, and, by extension, Poland's Communist Party, which is supposed to rule all walks of life. The strikers formed a committee to promulgate a list of demands which grew · and changed but always centered on the right to strike and to form independent unions.

The strikes revealed the extent of worker discontent. Poles are economically worse off than any of their counterparts in Eastern Europe, except for the Russians. Luxury goods that appear in Prague and East Berlin are not to be found in Warsaw. The average Polish wage earner gets 5,100 zlotys, or $178 a month. He waits 8 to 10 years for a new apartment, 3 to 4 years for a car. Life is an endless series of lines, for meat, for shoes, for gasoline and, lately, for newspapers.

To journalists covering Gdansk, several impressions stood out. The strike delegates were noticeably young, in their late 20's and early 30's. These were not wizened workers, burdened with unspeakable memories of the war years. They were not peasants-turned-workers, innately conservative and awed by authority and the amenities of urban living. They were a new generation in the Socialist world—well educated, articulate and angry.

Publicly, the workers reaffirmed their commitment to Socialism, but the feelings they expressed privately were reflected in a banner that read: "No Meat, No Bread, No Butter. All We Have To Eat Are the Words of Lenin."

Throughout, the call of nationalism and of the church was strong. It was no coincidence that the strikers' emblem was the national flag or that the Communist Internationale, sung on the first day, gave way to the historic Polish national anthem, "Poland Has Not Yet Perished." Masses were celebrated in the struck yard and the church's right to broadcast them every Sunday became a demand.

The Government watched, virtually helpless. When Gierek's paternalistic plea for a return to work was met with derision, ominous warnings were issued: The country was headed for disaster, perhaps even dissolution.

The protesters held firm. Twelve days after the strikers had shut the shipyard gates, they reopened them to admit the Government negotiators. The negotiations were piped over a loudspeaker system so that all the workers could follow them. While this innovation hampered give-and-take, it made for collective bargaining in a literal sense. The strike leaders' statements made it clear that the new movement was not just concerned with free trade unions; it was grappling with a fundamentally different vision of national life.

"We should think what led to this crisis," declared Andrzej Gwiazda, the most eloquent strike leader. "We must remember Marx's criticism of capitalism—that it was owners exploiting workers. For 35 years, we invest, we invest, we invest and our society has practically nothing to show for it. For years, people asked how much steel was being produced, how much coal was being dug. But nobody looked at what it all meant for the life of the workers."

Hearing these words, a Polish diplomat told a friend: "This country will never be the same. It's a turning point. We are witnessing the birth of the working class."

Five days later, when the message from Gdansk had mobilized workers all over the country—even the coal miners, who had not struck in 1956, 1970 or 1976, began walking out—the government capitulated.

For the signing of the historic accord, Lech Walesa produced a foot-long red and white pen, a souvenir of Pope John Paul II's visit last year. As he and First Deputy Prime Minister Jagielski scrawled their signatures, it towered over the bureaucrat's silver-plated ballpoint—a bit of lighthearted one-upmanship that delighted the victorious workers.

And yet, afterward, not all the strikers were jubilant. While some were satisfied with the progress that had been made—"We've broken down a barrier of fear," said a nurse at the Lenin Shipyard. "It's a great psychological achievement."—others had clearly wanted more.

A scholar who was one of the team of "experts" advising the strike committee ran into a cluster of workers who asked him what had happened to the demand for an end to censorship. The exhausted adviser explained that both sides had agreed that a modicum of censorship is necessary for the social good, and that the whole issue would be settled in a bill to be introduced within three months. The workers stared at him hostilely. A playwright who witnessed the scene recalls blurting out, without even thinking what he was saying, "There was no victory."

The continuing pressures for change are shaking almost all institutions. The Sejm (parliament), which has long been a rubber stamp, is now demanding real power. Research academies and universities are demanding greater autonomy. Students, a bit miffed that they missed out on all the action, are demanding an "independent" association to take the place of the party-dominated Socialist Students' Union.

Cultural life is changing. Journalists, writers, scholars and architects are forming a council that will challenge, among other things, the funding system by which the Ministry of Culture and Art hands out scholarships and stipends to party hacks. Polish films that had been blocked by the censors for years for being more political, graphically, than in their approved scripts, have started appearing on television. They are vivid portraits of the corruption, black-marketeering and exploitation that had so angered the strikers. Moviegoers have been shocked to see a never-before-released newsreel on the 1970 riots, showing tanks rumbling through the streets of Gdansk, militiamen advancing with drawn submachine guns, the Communist Party headquarters ransacked.

The press is gradually coming alive and fulfilling at least more of an informational role. But it is still carefully controlled by the

Government, mindful, no doubt, that in Czechoslovakia in 1968 a runaway press alarmed the Soviet Union, which promptly stamped out the "Prague Spring." Some intellectuals fear plans to codify precisely what can and cannot be printed may actually make the situation worse, since the Government may use the censorship law now being promulgated as a pretext to crack down on illegal literature, which has been unofficially tolerated.

The church, now regularly broadcasting Sunday masses on radio, is flexing its muscle. A joint church-Government commission has resumed talks on the long-standing list of demands of the Polish bishops. The church is in a strong bargaining position because, at the official level, it counseled moderation during the strikes, for which the Government is grateful, but in the Lenin Shipyard it showed itself as the single greatest institutional force in Poland.

The Communist Party itself is in disarray. In some of Poland's 49 provinces, local first secretaries are bucking change; in others, they are pressing for it, and in still others, they are vascillating. Party boss Kania, who has not yet fully consolidated his hold on power, sees his first priority as rebuilding the party, but that is no easy task. A half hearted purge against the corruption and privileges that accumulated in the Gierek era has begun, but because the abuses run so deep it is a tricky and almost self-defeating proposition; additional revelations would only further blacken the party's name.

To explain the August strikes, the evolving party rationalization is that "mistakes in policy," not theory, were to blame. Gierek had accumulated "too much power." The notion of independent unions is a Western one, but it is not incompatible with Socialism. This rationale has led to a Government propaganda campaign which by labeling political dissidents as "anti-Socialist elements" hopes to drive a wedge between them and the workers with whom they have struck up an alliance, the first such relationship in Eastern Europe. The new unions have made clear that any move against the dissidents would be unacceptable to them. For the time being, there is an uneasy standoff.

Over the long haul, whatever happens in Poland will be determined by the economy. And the economy appears headed for disaster. The country has a $21 billion foreign debt (owed to the

West), an amount so huge the 75 cents of every hard-currency dollar earned must go toward repaying it. Though the Poles have been insisting that they will repay on schedule, lately they have been giving out signs that they are not automatically against the idea of a moratorium.

What's more, the economic aspects of the Gdansk agreements, if carried out, will only make the situation worse. The wage and pension settlements will unleash a flood of new money at a time when there are few goods in the shops to absorb it—a classic recipe for discontent.

The effects of the agreement are already being felt in terms of declining production, brought on by such strike-won concessions as free Saturdays, longer maternity leaves and changes in the shift system in the mines. Most worrisome is the decrease in the excavation of coal, Poland's leading hard-currency earner. The Government is churning out figures to show that the manufacture of everything from machines to shoes is dropping, in an apparent campaign to switch the blame to work disruption caused by the unions. But because most people view the unions as instruments of constructive change, they are rejecting the Government's argument.

Under the weight of such practical dilemmas, the overriding theoretical question of whether independent trade unions are possible in a Communist country goes unnoticed. How can a command economy exist if the wage scales are not subject to command? How can central planners draw up five-year plans if officials must bargain year to year with Western-type unions? How can the party rule authoritatively if it doesn't rule in all spheres? One official, pressed on these questions, shrugged and said, "It almost sounds as impossible as a Communist Party existing side by side with the Catholic Church for 35 years."

There are now three sets of unions competing for 13 million Polish workers. The new, independent unions, operating under a national council known as Solidarity, now account for about eight million of that number. The old party-sponsored Central Council of Trade Unions and its fictionally autonomous branch unions, which are suffering mass desertions by construction and metal workers, doctors and teachers, account for the rest. A fierce struggle is under way for control of the vast array of services and funds once administered by the old unions—everything from sports clubs to holiday camps and statutory payments made for the death of a spouse or the birth of a child—which are now up for grabs.

For all their thunder, the new unions' power base is still mostly regional, on the Baltic coast, and they are weak in certain important industries, like the textile mills of Lodz, but they are certain to continue growing. They fiercely defend their right to accept contributions from Western trade unions, without which they would be unable to organize. The Government construes this as the kind of "outside interference" that could lend a pretext for Soviet involvement.

But the unions have not had extensive, ongoing contacts with Western labor organizations for advice and they have been chary of approaching Western embassies for assistance. Some West European governments and organizations have tried to provide what the unions need most—printing presses—but these have been stopped at the border.

On Oct. 3, the new unions, charging the Government with delay in implementing wage promises and biased news coverage, launched a one-hour strike. Its stunning success proved that the unions' strength was not a passing phenomenon. But some strikers felt the action was unnecessary and risky. A few began to question whether Lech Walesa—who has assumed the dimensions of a folk hero, but has also begun to show traces of demagoguery—has the intellectual capacity to lead the movement through a difficult phase of compromise, not combat.

Walesa has lost none of his zeal in moving from the role of an anonymous union activist to that of a worldwide media celebrity and, finally, at age 37, to being the undisputed leader of a burgeoning movement that while still rebellious is spawning its own bureaucracy. Solidarity is run by a staff of 20 and hundreds of volunteers out of a crumbly former hotel in Gdansk. Name and title cards—Chief, Propaganda Division, or Materials Division, or Press Division—run along a long corridor leading to the largest office, which is marked simply, "Lech Walesa, Chairman."

Walesa's organizing experience was gained in the streets, during the 1970 and 1976 riots. In 1976, when a delegate to the official trade union, he composed a list of workers' grievances and was fired from the Lenin Shipyard for being a political troublemaker. Two years later, he joined an underground committee to form free trade unions. In 1979, he was fired from a building company called Zremb, and last December, from an engineering firm called Elektromontaz, both times for political activities.

He is a complicated, private person, street smart, who rules by instinct. He openly enjoys such trappings of his high office as new suits and a new apartment, but draws the line at bigger benefits, which he considers corrupting. He claims to be put off by the adulation he receives but expects to get his way. He is deeply religious. A member of his entourage always carries a crucifix, to be fixed to the wall whenever Walesa addresses a gathering. His bodyguards carry Mace spray cans.

Because he has such a superstar following among the people, it is difficult to imagine someone rising up to challenge his leadership. His presence means that the tactics and direction of Solidarity depend to a considerable extent upon his own predilections, and this is unsettling because he is mercurial and constantly shifts between positions of moderation and militancy.

"He has good advisers," says Lech Badkowski, a member of the Gdansk union leadership, "but he doesn't listen to them—or rather he listens too much to them. Everything depends on who talks to him last."

During a remarkable campaignlike swing through the industrial south in mid-October, Walesa counseled moderation in declaring strikes. A week later, he was prepared to lead his organization in more sit-ins when the courts officially registered the new union but unilaterally rewrote its statutes to include a pledge to respect the "leading role" of the Communist Party. Under the influence of the Gdansk leadership, reluctant delegates from other parts of the country were pressed into proclaiming selective strikes scheduled for Wednesday if the Government doesn't override the court ruling.

Walesa's moderate side emerges after he has consulted with church officials, including Stefan Cardinal Wyszynski, the aging and powerful primate of Poland. The militant Mr. Hyde aspect of his nature becomes dominant after strategy sessions with Jacek Kuron, of KOR, a principal adviser.

Another possible showdown between the new unions and the authorities lies ahead. What it could produce in the shape of awful consequences was driven home to Poles by the coincidence of a Warsaw Pact Foreign Ministers meeting in Warsaw in mid-October, a reminder, not that any was needed, that Poland is inextricably bound in a military alliance to other bloc countries.

For the moment, the Soviet Union has accepted the independent unions as the price its troublesome ally had to pay to extract itself from chaos. But Moscow clearly regards the union movement as a Trojan horse capable of spreading heresy throughout the Socialist empire, and it expects the Polish party to control it.

At a hurriedly arranged meeting in the Kremlin on Oct. 30, Polish Communist Party boss Kania appeared to have won Soviet backing for his handling of the labor crisis so far, but how solid that backing is and how long it will last is problematical.

The Kremlin's concern is that the contagion will spread beyond Poland's borders. Moscow has resumed jamming Western broadcasts but it can do little about the 600-meter-high antenna of Warsaw Radio One. The only dissident connection in the Soviet bloc is between Poland and Czechoslovakia, where activists have traditionally maintained sporadic clandestine contact. Czechoslovakia, which sarcastically called the Polish dissidents "godfathers of the new unions," has been arresting its own dissidents.

The strikes in Poland have set off unsettling ripples in other East European countries, whose economies are troubled by a rising inflation that puts consumer goods out of reach. Even before Poland's labor problems erupted this summer, there were reports of strikes in both the Soviet Union and Rumania, and the head of Hungary's official trade-union movement admitted recently that "work stoppages" had occurred there, too. Strikes were also reported to have taken place early in October in Tartu, Estonia, a region of perennial discontent. The possibility cannot be ruled out that other strikes, unreported as of yet, have happened elsewhere in the bloc.

Erich Honecker, the East German leader, Nicolae Ceausescu, Rumania's party chief, and Vasil Bilak, a prominent Czechoslovakian Communist Party official, have all criticized developments in Poland in increasingly strident tones. Ominously, Czechoslovakia, the most doctrinaire Soviet satellite since its dissidents were quieted in 1968, offered to send "aid" to true-blooded Polish Communists fighting reactionary forces.

The Brezhnev Doctrine, as it was expounded by Pravda to justify the Warsaw-Pact invasion of Czechoslovakia, holds that no ruling Communist Party has the right to "damage Socialism in its own country, nor the fundamental interests of other Socialist countries, nor the worldwide workers' movement." The defining feature of the "Prague Spring" was that the Czech Party itself took a runaway turn deemed menacing by Moscow.

This is not the case in Poland. The party is not heretical; it continually reaffirms its loyalty to Moscow, and it is doing all it can to contain the situation. The question is: Is it strong enough? The single greatest fear of a long-experienced Polish journalist, who is no friend to the system, is that the party's prestige in the Kremlin has sunk too low. In the final analysis, he explains, only the party is a buffer against Soviet intervention. The same thought is captured in a popular new Polish saying that plays upon Vanya, the Russian diminutive for Ivan: "Better Kania than Vanya."

Since 1956, Poland has not been, properly speaking, a Soviet satellite; its orbit has been a bit too elliptical. The pull from the West is strong: from France, with its historical and cultural ties; from West Germany, the despised World War II occupier, now the major non-Socialist trading partner, and from the United States, where 10 million Polish-Americans constitute the largest group in the diaspora called "Polonia."

Despite Poland's strategic and industrial importance to the Kremlin, the Soviets have been reluctant to put to a test the extent of Polish loyalty to Soviet hegemony.

Only in Poland do Government officials take pains to draw elaborate distinctions between nationalism—construed as a negative, backward sentiment—and patriotism—the acceptable face of the same emotion—because only in Poland is nationalism so clearly seen as threatening the Soviet relationship. In East Germany,

Soviet troops are as common as lampposts. In Poland, the 30,000 Soviet troops have to be garrisoned out of sight. When Leonid Brezhnev places an obligatory wreath on the Tomb of the Unknown Soldier in Warsaw's Victory Square, he is well aware that the soldier died during the Russo-Polish War of 1920.

Polish nationalism has grown, not diminished, under Communism. One reason is that it was plastered over with historical lies. The two greatest official taboo subjects are the secret Hitler-Stalin pact to partition Poland in 1939 and the Katyn Forest massacre, in which Stalin's secret police liquidated more than 10,000 Polish Army officers in 1940. These facts, taught in every Polish home, are kept alive because they are not acknowledged, and when the anniversaries roll around, they are commemorated.

A second reason is that Poles, more than Czechs or Hungarians or East Germans, are convinced that their economic ties to the Soviet Union are exploitative. To some extent, the conviction is outmoded, a memory of the postwar years when Poland was forced to deliver up various products at fractional "fraternal" prices. It ignores the fact that 80 percent of Poland's oil comes from the Soviet Union, at less than world-market prices. But the public perception is still there. Many Poles believe that there is a meat shortage because the best cuts are shipped off to Moscow, whereas most of the ham, pork and sausage that is exported goes to the United States and Western Europe, to obtain hard currency.

Whether the Polish leadership admits it or not, anti-Russian nationalism is its trump card. The Soviets will not invade, the theory goes, because the Poles, unlike the Czechs, would fight back. The international cost would simply be too high. What the theory ignores, and what some people fear, is Moscow's capacity for "soft" intervention by making common cause with hard-line Polish party elements that now stand purged but could return to power with a vengeance. The Soviet Union could easily destabilize any section of the country and use the pretext of social disorder for sponsoring a change in government.

Because the stakes are so high, few people doubt that Russia would use outright military force if she felt her own stability was truly threatened. This could happen if the Polish Communist Party lost all semblance of control or if the strikes spread to the nearby

Soviet republic of Byelorussia or into the Ukraine, or to other Socialist countries. If force were used, Soviet troops would have to do much of the job on their own. East German soldiers, evoking war memories, would bring on an instant rebellion. Poland's armed forces (317,500 regular troops, 95,000 paramilitary) would certainly not fire upon Polish citizens, though they might very well turn their guns against any invaders.

The question then becomes: How would the West react? The United States has made it clear that it would not intervene because Poland, after all, is in the Soviet Union's sphere of influence. But the political pressures for some sort of response, if only covert arms supplies, would be considerable. The possibility of a major East-West confrontation would then be very large—indeed.

Poland is accustomed to compromise—no word better describes its national life since the end of World War II. In each of the three previous workers' revolts, the gains were short-lived and the promises broken, but never did the level of repression slide back to what it had been before. The current revolt has gone much further than any of the others. Suddenly, it seems to be all or nothing. There is a sense that a line has been crossed, a historic, exciting, but dangerous line.

"I am afraid in my bones," says a Polish writer, "that we shall have to pay dearly for those few days in August."

POLAND'S ECONOMIC DISASTER[3]

A Western visitor arriving in Poland might wonder at first what the talk of economic crisis is all about. From the plane he sees smoke billowing from factory chimneys and tower cranes at work on new high-rise office buildings and apartment blocks. On the way into Warsaw from the airport he encounters swarms of darting cars, driven with the traditional dash of the Polish cavalry. On the street he sees well-nourished people dressed in studied ap-

[3]Reprint of an article by Robert Ball, staff writer. *Fortune*. 104:42–8. S. 7, '81. Reprinted from the September 7, 1981 issue of Fortune Magazine by special permission. Copyright © 1981 by Time Inc.

proximations of Western styles. At his hotel, as modern and comfortable as many at home, he is offered bacon and eggs for breakfast, plus a lavish assortment of cold cuts.

Just around the corner, however, he meets the reality of Polish daily life in the form of endless and nearly motionless lines of shoppers waiting outside food stores in the hope of buying modest rations of meat, sugar, flour, and other necessities. Similar queues stretch away in front of kiosks and shops selling cigarettes, bread, canned goods, coffee, milk, butter, toothpaste, soap, automotive spare parts, or almost anything else Westerners take for granted. Even a visitor hardened to the frustrations of Eastern Europe— the haphazard service, the nonfunctioning faucet, the instant dilapidation—has never seen anything like this. Everything people need is in short supply.

The queues are the visible manifestation of the worst economic disaster to befall any European country since the devastation of World War II. Poland's economic crisis is crucially linked to a major continuing political crisis for the Russians. The outcome is going to be important, not only because of the possibility that the Soviet Union will send in troops, but also because what happens will have much to do with shaping the future of Moscow's whole system of satellites. In this article, *Fortune* examines the economic underpinnings of Poland's plight, and the outlook.

A Wrongheaded Policy

In the past three years, Poland's gross national product has diminished by nearly a quarter. Output may fall 17% this year alone, and bottom has not been touched. Farm and industrial production have collapsed. At a time when the population is flush with cash and clamoring for goods, Polish industry is operating at something like 75% of a capacity that, fully utilized, was barely able to provide essential supplies. Farmers count themselves lucky if they can feed their families.

The reasons for this collapse, severe enough to threaten the stability of the country, are to be found in an economic policy so wrongheaded that it surpasses understanding. Poland has a skilled labor force, much good farmland, and an abundance of mineral wealth. But the Communist leaders starved agriculture and light industry in order to squander the nation's own resources and at least $27 billion borrowed in the West on grandiose heavy-industrial projects—often requiring imports of expensive Western technology. The utility of these projects for the Polish economy was often doubtful, and now they have turned into catastrophes.

Take, for example, former Party Secretary Edward Gierek's pet project, the new steel mill in his native Katowice. This immense complex, designed to pour ten million tons of steel a year (or almost half as much as all of U.S. Steel's mills turned out last year) was built at a cost of more than 160 billion zlotys (nearly $5 billion at the tourist exchange rate of 33.68 zlotys to the dollar). Additional billions went to build a railway to bring the iron ore from the Russian border. The Katowice mill is producing only around four million tons of steel a year, some sort of record for poor return on investment.

Or take the 1974 licensing agreement under which the Ursus Tractor Works near Warsaw was to make a light tractor designed by Massey-Ferguson. Almost $1 billion was sunk into this effort, and instead of the planned 75,000 tractors a year, the factory is building only 500. The package of imported components for each tractor costs $6,500 in hard currency. Ursus is not licensed to sell the tractors in the West, and in Communist countries the model can't be sold at a price that would recover the cost. In addition, the specifications are not metric and nothing made elsewhere in Poland fits the tractor. The Ursus management has hopes of adapting the design to use all-Polish components, but that will require another $800 million or so.

These examples can stand for countless similar ones in the chemical, automobile, electronics, and other key industries. The vaunted opening of Polish industry to Western technology created a dependence on imports of components and equipment that only the West can supply, but without a matching growth in production of goods that could be exported in exchange for hard currency. In its present strapped condition, Poland can no longer import the components. The result is that costly plants stand idle, but the meter is still running: the work force cannot be laid off because of the government's ideological commitment to full employment.

Where production is not dependent on Western components, other horrors loom. Coal output, worth its weight in foreign exchange, is down from a perhaps fictitious peak of 200 million tons in 1979 to around 160 million tons this year. The current level of output is just enough to meet domestic requirements, with nothing left for export. Professor Jan Mujzel, head of the state planning institute, expects power shortages next winter; in July, 1981 some power stations had only two to three days' supply of coal.

A Planning Failure

While mineral resources were exploited at a rate that would have shamed a robber baron, production of vital goods languished. Refusal to consider profitability or the requirements of the market led to the setting up of hundreds of factories turning out at exorbitant cost things about as salable as left shoes, such as those overpriced Massey tractors.

One shortage leads to another. The country is short half a million vehicular batteries, about six months' normal production. The shortage of batteries—and of tires—keeps thousands of farm tractors rusting in the sheds and out of the fields. The farm economy has also been hit by a lack of fertilizers, herbicides, and animal feeds. And all this in a system that calls itself a planned economy.

The postwar economic history of Poland is an almost uninterrupted sequence of blunders committed in the name of planning. Successive crises sparked unrest in 1956, 1968, 1970, 1976, and 1980; in 1956 and 1970, hundreds of Poles were killed when security forces fired on demonstrators. To blame this sorry record on persistent "distortions" of Communist doctrine, as successive Polish governments have tried to do, is like blaming Soviet grain shortages on 64 years of bad weather. More than anything else, the party's mismanagement of the national economy has demonstrated its incompetence and discredited it in Polish eyes.

Against this background, the events of 1980 unfolded. Trouble started, as so often before, over a sudden increase in the price of meat as the government struggled yet again to match supply and demand. At the Lenin shipyard in Gdansk, a hitherto-unknown electrician named Lech Walesa became a national hero by leading strikes initially aimed at rolling back the price increase, or gaining an equivalent wage boost. The strikes soon became political and eventually led to the historic Gdansk agreement. For the first time in any Communist state, the striking workers gained the right to organize themselves in an independent trade union, Solidarity, and the right to strike.

While the Polish United Workers' Party (PUWP), the supposed vanguard of the working class, watched helplessly, millions of workers deserted the official trade unions, and the PUWP itself lost 300,000 members. Solidarity is now a national movement with ten million dues-paying members. It dwarfs the 2.7-million-member PUWP, not to mention the official unions, which have virtually withered away. In a typical enterprise, Solidarity represents 80% or more of the employees.

The hapless Gierek was replaced as First Secretary by Stanislaw Kania, a squat, unimposing *apparatchik* whose security-service background initially commended him to Moscow. Kania, however, ruled out the use of force and proclaimed a willingness to negotiate. On every disputed issue Solidarity got its way—the terms of registration of the new organization, limits on censorship, access to the media, the right to publish a national weekly and local newsletters, the creation of Rural Solidarity as an organization representing peasants. As one Western diplomat in Warsaw says wonderingly, "Solidarity is still batting a thousand."

Solidarity has had support from another power center, the Roman Catholic church. In Poland the Catholic faith is inextricably linked with patriotism: it was the church that kept the idea of nationhood alive through the entire 19th century, after the country was partitioned by Russia, Prussia, and the Austro-Hungarian Empire. The PUWP, alone among ruling Communist parties, accepts practicing Catholics as members.

Political acumen acquired by the church in decades of stubborn defense against party encroachment has rubbed off on Solidarity. A new and untried organization in which—Poles being Poles—emotions and aspirations run high, Solidarity has so far not once allowed itself to be provoked into rash moves. It has chosen its ground and its issues carefully, has wielded its potent strike weapon judiciously, and has scrupulously avoided actions or statements that could be taken as anti-Soviet or anti-Socialist.

A Terse Telegram

When the PUWP congress confirmed the centrist tandem of Kania and Prime Minister Wojciech Jaruzelski in their top party posts, Brezhnev sent Kania a terse telegram of congratulation. But despite what appears to be a breathing spell, the shadow of Soviet military intervention may never disappear completely. If food riots were to become so widespread as to cause a breakdown of public order, or if Solidarity and the authorities became locked in a duel to the death, the Soviet leaders might well risk action.

The Russians may have felt that the outcome of the PUWP congress could have been worse. Though for the first time the delegates were elected by secret ballot from rival slates of nominees, the hopes of the more radical reformers were disappointed. The sense of the congress was a reaffirmation of the centrist line of *odnowa,* or renewal. This involves the continuing acceptance of the role of "society"—the party code word for Solidarity and the church—as partners of the PUWP in national life.

Such sharing of power is unprecedented in a Communist state. But Solidarity apparently is too strong to be ignored. Now it must decide how and when to apply its power. Anyone who has attended a meeting of Solidarity delegates knows that there are almost as many views on what should be done as there are members of the organization.

One who believes the time has come to cool the hotter heads is Lech Walesa. "What we need is less striking and protesting and more working and monitoring the agreements that have been signed," he told *Fortune.* "We should not be in a hurry. We still have to agree on our own program and elect our governing bodies." His view of what the composition of his organization's governing bodies should be was stated last month in a brief, forceful speech to 500 Solidarity delegates from the Gdansk region. He urged the replacement of eight out ot ten people on the presidium he heads. Said he, "I need around me fewer people who want to fight all the time and more who want to talk and negotiate."

Walesa wants to mold the many local agreements into a national one that could serve as a uniform "workers' charter." He hopes to agree with the government on draft legislation dealing with economic reform, union rights, worker self-management, and limitation of censorship. Walesa's views on censorship are surprisingly conservative: "We even say that a little bit of censorship is needed, because some publications are put out in our name which are not controlled by us."

Whatever happens, Poles are going to have to accept a drop in their standard of living, because it will take time to get the economy straightened out. A major source of friction could be Solidarity's insistence that worker self-management should include giving employees an important say in appointing heads of enterprises. In addition, increasing the efficiency of the Polish economy implies some reduction in the present grotesque overmanning of enterprises—a prospect almost equally dismaying to the government and to Solidarity. The Ursus tractor plant, for example, employs 16,500 people, plus 8,000 in sub-plants, to turn out 55,000 Polish-designed tractors annually—about $2\frac{1}{4}$ tractors per employee per year. If the Poles could get their new Massey-Ferguson production line operating as it should, 8,000 workers would turn out nearly ten tractors a year each.

The 24-hour Industry

The government is seeking to combine a wage freeze with whopping price increases. Though average earnings are less than $200 a month, money wages have outpaced the growth of productivity for years, and this imbalance has been exacerbated by the 20% to 25% wage boosts won by Solidarity in the last year, when output was falling sharply. As Zygmunt Szeliga, deputy editor of the weekly newspaper *Polityka*, puts it, "Printing banknotes is the only Polish industry working 24 hours a day."

In a normal economy, consumer prices would have zoomed; in Poland's command economy, queues lengthened. The government is now determined to claw back some of the huge overhang in purchasing power by raising prices. Professor Zdzislaw Krasinski, head of the Price Commission, says food prices "have been totally artificial," and he wants to push them up in three or four steps between now and early 1982. The price of a two-pound loaf of bread will more than double, going from 20 cents to 50 cents.

Overall, the cost of food will rise by around 120%. Eliminating subsidies on everything but milk is expected to save $10 billion a year in public expenditure, nearly wiping out the budget deficit. Though some of the increases will be passed on to farmers to encourage production, the main purpose, according to Krasinski, is to reduce food consumption 8% to 10%. The hefty hike in food prices will be accompanied on January 1, 1982 by a similar rise in raw-material and energy prices (coal will go from around $15 to $80 per ton) and abolition of preferential prices for industrial as against private use (gasoline, for example, is sold to industrial enterprises for less than half the $2.62 per gallon it costs motorists).

However necessary, these cannot be popular measures. Solidarity leaders recognize the need for price increases, but want to see them as part of a broader program of reform promising a long-term economic improvement. The government's declared intent is to change the old rigid party-controlled system of central direction and central allocation of raw materials and investment credits.

The new system would be one in which the managers of enterprises run their own affairs, set their own prices, pay wages and buy materials out of their own earnings, and make capital investments from retained profits or by taking bank loans on commercial terms. Enterprises needing hard currency for imports would bid for it against other claimants. Says Jan Mujzel, the planning-institute boss, a member of Solidarity, "I don't believe central planners can allocate foreign exchange intelligently among enterprises."

Poles Can Still Joke

So far, so reasonable. But can the old dogs of Polish industry be taught these new tricks? Central allocation of scarce materials to selected industries is to continue for a transition period of uncertain length. Getting efficiency through competition is hard in a country like Poland where there may be only one producer of refrigerators or TV sets. And closing down uneconomic enterprises would require retraining and redeploying workers, a major task for which little visible preparation has been made. Eugeniusz Dobosz, head of the employment department in the Ministry of Labor, says blithely, "We don't need a program for unemployment. If we overcome the crisis, there will be no unemployment problem." No wonder Poles joke that *odnowa* (renewal) is really *od nowo* (here we go again).

Bad as the economic situation is, miracles are not required to put Poland on its feet. Some enterprises, such as the Baltic shipyards, are already operating efficiently. The Lenin Shipyard in Gdansk, where worker discontent gave birth to Solidarity, has increased output 35% in the last year, and annual exports of the yard are running more than $300 million. Klemens Gniech, boss of the enterprise, says his order books are full through 1984.

This year's big jump in output is being achieved despite a cut in the shipyard's workweek from six days to five. Gains in productivity have fully covered hefty wage increases. Gniech, an engineer appointed by the old regime, allies himself with Solidarity. Says he: "I accept Solidarity's program in its entirety and I hope the party does too. There is no other way out." Each week he meets with employee representatives to hear their gripes and suggestions and to keep them informed about what is going on. The meetings deal in the main with routine shop-floor grievances, but Gniech says the program of communication and consultation "creates the right atmosphere."

In industry generally, simply getting back to work and avoiding grandiose investment schemes would bring improvement. Present shortages are due less to the shorter hours won by Solidarity than to a for-lack-of-a-nail progression in which a dearth of certain components, often imported from the West, has paralyzed normal work. Assuming a final agreement on rescheduling Poland's foreign debt, the West would be well advised to help overcome bottlenecks by advancing enough new credit to enable Poland to import crucial items not available from the Soviet bloc. Such a modest aid program—it might be called a "Marszalkowska Plan," after the name of Warsaw's principal shopping street— would be chicken feed by international lending standards. But chicken feed, both figuratively and literally, is a commodity Poland badly needs right now.

In agriculture, too, the outlook permits hope. Thanks to good weather, the 1981 harvest should be the best in years. Some 80% of Poland's farms are still privately owned, and these farms are more efficient than the state farms despite the tiny size of most private land holdings—85% are 25 acres or less. Output could be vastly expanded if the peasants could get the fertilizer, fodder, and equipment they need—and if their own morale could be lifted. They have been demoralized in the words of Zygmunt Szeliga of *Polityka,* by "30 years of policy zigzags depending on whether ideology or the supply situation was considered more important." The government will have to convince the peasants that this time it means what it says about accepting that ownership of land. Self-sufficiency in food would transform the balance of payments. 50% of Poland's imports from the West this year were agricultural products.

Despite its fulminations, the Soviet Union, which supplies 70% of Poland's raw materials, is helping to ease the economic bind. According to Zbigniew Karcz, head of the foreign department in the Polish Finance Ministry, the Russians loaned Poland $1.1 billion in hard currency between September 1980 and last March [1981]. Moreover, the Russians have boosted deliveries of oil and other products and have indicated willingness to let Poland run a deficit in trade between the two countries; the deficit will amount to $1.5 billion this year and is likely to continue at that level. Karcz thinks the goods are better than more hard-currency loans: "What we need are goods that we can repay with other goods later on."

Poland must look both East and West. Stanislaw Albinowski, an influential economist, says: "We must have trade with the West to be able to service our debt, and we must have trade with the East for our raw materials." The urgent problem is to get wheels turning and supplies to the populace. This will require not only a great national effort, but also "fraternal assistance" in the good sense from Communist parties—and from Western countries whose ties with Poland go back a good deal further.

EDITOR'S INTRODUCTION

As the power of the Polish workers' movement grew and the government was forced to accede to more and more of their demands, the question that preoccupied all Western observers was whether the Soviet government could tolerate the existence of a democratic institution within its sphere of influence. Close ties between Poland and the West, confirmed by the visits of U.S. Presidents Nixon, Ford, and Carter in 1972, 1975, and 1977 respectively, were cited by the Kremlin as the cause of social unrest with the Soviet bloc, but to Western political analysts such as Walter Laqueur it seemed that the Communist system was beginning to show "the internal contradictions which must eventually destroy it."

The U.S. governments of Carter and Reagan studiously avoided taking any action that might exacerbate Soviet fears, and limited their public support for the Poles to the wish that they might be allowed to resolve their domestic problems without interference. President Carter approved new credit guarantees for the bankrupt Polish economy in September 1980, and in April of the following year President Reagan authorized the sale of basic food supplies, accepting payment in virtually worthless Polish currency. Numerous American and European labor movements also gave assistance to the Polish people.

Why did the West act so cautiously, avoiding any action that might have given practical assistance to the cause of Polish democracy? The four articles in this section provide some answers to that question, pointing out from their various political standpoints that West and East alike had a vital interest in the peaceful resolution of the crisis. Seweryn Bialer of Columbia University, writing in *Foreign Affairs,* argues that if the Polish turmoil led to a Soviet invasion, the consequences for international relations would be incalculable. Ronald Steel, in an article from the *New Republic,* states that "the harsh reality is that the superpowers have a vested interest in the status quo [in Poland]." Writing in *Commentary,* Walter Laqueur takes a notably different view, arguing that the West should not assist in perpetuating a repressive political order by extending further monetary assistance to the Poles. In an article from *Foreign Policy,* Dimitri Simes of Johns Hopkins University counsels prudence and advocates a policy that will encourage, but not insist upon, greater flexibility within the Soviet system.

POLAND AND THE SOVIET IMPERIUM[1]

Poles! If you cannot prevent your neighbors from devouring your nation, make it impossible for them to digest it.
— Jean-Jacques Rousseau

Events in Poland since August 1980, the struggle of Polish workers for their rights, constitute a critical turning point in the history of the Soviet imperium. The situation, still completely unpredictable at the onset of the new year, holds much more importance for the future of the world communist movement, the Soviet empire, and the Soviet Union itself than the Hungarian Revolution of 1956, the Polish revolt of the same year, the Czechoslovak reforms of 1968, and even the Stalin-Tito rupture of 1947–48. Its international implications are no less grave. Poland is the key country in the Soviet bloc in terms of strategic location, military and economic potential, and size of population. A major lasting change there could transform, if not destroy, the Soviet Union's East European empire.

Even before the recent events, Poland was far from being a typical East European communist state. It is the only communist country in which individual small landholders form the vast majority of the peasantry. The Polish Catholic Church represents a

[1]Reprint of an article by Seweryn Bialer, Professor of Political Science at Columbia University and Director of its Research Institute on International Change. *Foreign Affairs.* 59:522–39. Ap. '81. Reprinted by permission from *Foreign Affairs,* America and the World 1980. Copyright © 1981 by the Council on Foreign Relations, Inc.

virtual alternate government with a moral authority unmatched by any postwar Polish regime. (As a Vatican joke has it, the most Catholic countries in the world are Poland, Ireland and the Vatican, in that order.) Culturally, Poland belongs to the West; its cities exhibit a lifestyle that is Western in character.

It is a homogeneous country of intense national consciousness and deep national pride, with a long tradition of struggle for independence, and of survival under the most adverse conditions of foreign oppression. Even with Soviet troops on the ground, the communist takeover of 1944–45 was resisted in what was for a time a virtual civil war. Since then, 35 years of communist rule have failed to eradicate the distinct national identity shared by all strata of society and expressed by an intelligentsia whose very label is synonymous with dissent. In recent years, numerous dissident organizations have been able to communicate their views to a broad range of publics; hundreds of thousands of students took part in so-called flying universities, where professors taught courses they could not present at the regular universities. And industrial workers have confronted security forces in the streets on three occasions in the last quarter-century (1956, 1970, 1976) to demonstrate their opposition to the regime.

What has happened in Poland since the labor unrest in August 1980 is too well known to require detailed review. The crisis began with local strikes against price increases. A workers' movement quickly rose and spread across the nation, and a series of broadly based sit-in strikes in factories and mines forced the government, under the threat of a general strike, to promise the workers the right—unprecedented in a communist regime—to organize an independent trade union movement. Other demands, political in nature, were raised in the process, and hard-pressed Polish leaders promised to overhaul the regime, the policymaking process, and the policies themselves. The workers' struggle brought about the resignation of Polish Party leader Edward Gierek as well as the almost complete replacement of the upper echelons of the Party and the government. What took place in Poland during the past few months is nothing less, to use the words of Karl Marx, than the transformation of the Polish working class from *eine Klasse in sich* to *eine Klasse für sich*. (A rough translation would be: "from a class in itself [within the system] into a class for itself.")

Why did the workers' strikes in Poland assume such massive proportions? Why did the workers' demands concentrate on relatively far-reaching structural changes, so exceptional for a communist state? Obviously events were triggered by the price increases which the Polish government announced during the late summer. But just as obviously, the reasons underlying those events are much deeper and broader.

First of all, by the late 1970s, it had become evident, not only to the Polish working class but to the population as a whole, that Poland faced nothing less than the collapse of its planning and management system and the total bankruptcy of its economy. An examination of recent trends in Polish economic development provides indisputable evidence for this conclusion.

In 1980, it is quite clear, the national income of Poland showed for the second consecutive year an absolute decline, a dubious honor not achieved by any other Soviet bloc country. Not only are there immense shortages in the supply of necessities—which, because of their immediate short-range political implications, have received the greatest attention in the press—but of even greater significance are enormous disruptions in the industrial, construction and agrarian sectors. These trends have long-range implications for a Polish economy already burdened by massive hard-currency indebtedness.

In the months of August and September alone, according to official estimates, industrial production dropped 17 percent below that of the same period in 1979. Total production losses for the July-September period are estimated in the neighborhood of $2.3 billion. For the coal-mining industry, one of the mainstays of the Polish economy, the shortfall may be as large as ten percent of the total output. In the first three quarters of 1980, the plan for the construction industry was fulfilled by only 37 percent. The grain harvest, which was about 21.3 million tons in 1978, declined to 17.3 million tons in 1979, and mounted, according to optimistic estimates, to just over 19 million tons in 1980. This total is officially declared to be eight million tons below current needs, thus requiring expensive, large-scale imports. Meat production, which was 3.3 million tons in 1979, may have declined to 2.4 million tons in 1980 and may not exceed 2.2 million tons in 1981. The potato harvest is officially estimated to have been the worst in 20 years, down almost 40 percent from that of 1979.

What went so wrong with the Polish economy? One key cause can be traced to the critical decision made by Gierek in 1970 when he replaced the discredited Party chief, Wladyslaw Gomulka. Workers' unrest, prompted by dissatisfaction with the economic situation, had led to Gomulka's overthrow. Gierek promised to improve the situation radically. He could have chosen to restructure the Polish economy and reform its unwieldy and cumbersome planning, management and incentive system. In doing so, he would have had to rely upon long-range recovery and improvement of the Polish economy. Instead, he elected a different course. His strategy combined significant imports of Western technology, financed on credit, with heavy investments in the growth of Polish industry. The theory was that massive infusions of Western technology would permit Poland to switch from extensive to intensive growth; and foreign debts incurred in the process could be repaid by the consequent increase in exports from a revitalized Polish industry.

If the policy initially yielded positive results, in the last analysis it failed to meet expectations. In the years 1971–75, the net industrial product increased, according to official statistics, at the rate of almost 11 percent per year; that is to say, about 30 percent faster than in the preceding decade. Real industrial wages, which from 1961 to 1970 grew at 1.8 percent per year, rose in the 1971–75 period by 7.2 percent annually.

But from the mid-1970s Gierek's program foundered. Unforeseen world economic conditions combined with weaknesses in the preparation and execution of Gierek's policy to slow economic development and erode Poland's ability to meet its credit obligations. First, the energy crisis increased radically the cost of oil required for development. Second, the recession in the West impeded the sale of Polish goods in hard-currency markets, thus dissolving Gierek's hope that expanded exports would repay foreign debts. Third, the investment policy to the Gierek government proved ill conceived and unrealistic. At some stages as much as 40 percent of the Polish national income was devoted to investment, about 75 percent of this being devoted to heavy and export industries; increasing domestic demand was left unsatisfied, thus creating immense inflationary pressures and making Poland dependent on expensive imports. Fourth, and most important, the government did not undertake any of the major reforms in the system of planning and management which might have prepared the system to cope with the demands arising from increased dependence on intensive growth, the application of new technology, and the growth of productivity.

Enormous disproportions and bottlenecks resulted from the rapid economic growth sustained by credits and imports. The proportion of unfinished investment projects grew rapidly; the utilization of foreign technology was highly inefficient and its diffusion slow. Beyond a short-range impact, the major inflow of Western technology failed to generate significant long-term improvements in productivity. The import of technology and credits could not serve as a substitute for structural reforms. The structural mismanagement of the economy became endemic and visible to everyone; waste assumed incredible proportions.

During the first years of Gierek's program, the expectations of the Polish working class soared. Those expectations were satisfied in part—at least initially. By 1979 and 1980, however, the situation had become dangerously unstable. In the face of diminishing economic returns from an increasingly stagnant economy, consumers experienced both inflation and severe shortages of basic commodities. That the Gierek leadership lacked credibility in economic matters had become patently obvious. As the same time the government neither informed the people about the true economic situation nor adequately prepared them for the necessary austerity measures. The belief spread throughout all sectors of society, including the Party itself, that the economic system had outlived its usefulness, that it had nothing more to offer—in short, that it was bankrupt.

Poland's economic crisis paralleled a crisis of political authority as the Party become totally divorced from the realities of everyday Polish life and its inner life stagnated. United under Gierek's command, the Party leadership allowed no fresh voices to pose

questions concerning the relationship between the Party and the
working class or the state and the economy—or if such voices were
raised, they were quickly silenced. After 35 years of communist
rule in Poland, and Polish population, including the working
class, ceased to believe in the Party's authority, its ability, and its
right to rule. Nothing so clearly demonstrated the gulf between
the legal and the civil society as the overwhelming popular response to the visit of Pope John Paul II to his native country in
the summer of 1979.

The effects of virtual economic bankruptcy and the crisis of
political authority were compunded for the population by a
heightened visibility and awareness of official corruption and
privilege. Workers harbored a growing sense of the injustice per-
petrated by a state which claimed incessantly to represent the
workers and stressed continuously in its propaganda the centrality
of the workers in society. When shortages of foodstuffs developed,
no system of rationing spread the burden evenly. The hated symbol of elite privilege was the so-called yellow curtain store which
concealed from public view the sale of scarce goods to the Party
and state bureaucracy. Another source of aggravation was the
newly opened shops that traded only with foreign currency.

Disaffection among workers found other sources of nourish-
ment. Plans for investment in public housing were not fulfilled.
The housing situation became critical, especially for young working couples who wished to marry and had to wait many years for
an apartment. Mobility into the middle class was felt to be more
and more difficult for the children of working people, as the higher
education system, the major channel of mobility, did not expand
rapidly. All in all, there developed within the working class a deep
sense of just social grievance against the system that ruled in its
name, a sense of grievance that was no longer responsive to reas-
surances and promises from the Party leadership.

A final and crucial reason helps explain the scale of labor unrest: the character of the Polish working class itself had changed.
The authorities failed to grasp the fact that a new working class
had emerged. The peasants who flocked to the factories in the
1950s and 1960s improved their economic and cultural lot by the
very act of becoming urbanized. Now no longer dominated by

peasant recruits, the Polish working class is urban in origin, and has a different attitude and a different set of expectations. Moreover, it is not burdened politically by the paralyzing memory of Stalinist terror. More self-assured and willing to take risks, it is more activist. And it differs culturally from its predecessor. This generation of workers is better educated and better trained than the previous generation, and enjoys a new sense of confidence and self-identity. Finally, the workers are better able to compare their own conditions with those of workers in the West or in more developed East European countries. They listen to foreign radio broadcasts; they talk with millions of tourists visiting Poland; and hundreds of thousands—even millions—of them travel abroad. It was this new working class which, in the developing situation of last summer, undertook to redress its grievances and demand social justice. . . . While we do not know the full extent of the gains already won by the workers, some of these gains represent significant concessions that will endure. This consideration alone warrants posing the question: Why did the workers win in Poland?

To begin with, the workers' challenge to the communist regime was much more difficult to counter than the previous eruptions to which dissident intellectuals accustomed communist regimes in the post-Stalin era. A massive movement of workers in a so-called workers' state is qualitatively different from a numerically small movement of the intelligentsia which can be successfully managed by combining intimidation, repression, bribery and forced emigration.

Second, consider the way the struggle developed, and the general political situation in Poland. Polish workers learned from the experiences of 1956, 1970 and 1976 when their confrontations with the authorities in street demonstrations turned quickly into violence and defeat. In 1980, they adopted a new tactic that was much more effective. Sit-in strikes and occupation of factories put the onus of initiating violence in any effort to eject the workers—a difficult task in itself—on the government. The workers exhibited an admirable measure of self-discipline, a high degree of organization, and an unprecedented ability to act in concert.

Third, for the first time in Polish history the two streams of opposition to the regime became effectively joined—the broad workers' movement and a widespread movement of dissident intellectuals. Their union is symbolized by the commissions of experts attached to the newly formed free-trade unions. The role of the dissident intelligentsia in these events should not be exaggerated. The main force behind these events was an authentic, spontaneous working-class movement; the dissident intelligentsia jumped on the bandwagon. They did add an important dimension, however, by supplying advice and, even more important, by providing the communications network through which news of the workers' actions reached the country. The ability of workers along the coast to communicate their actions and demands to workers in other parts of Poland and to the population in general was a key element in forcing the retreat of the government, which faced not simply a localized strike but the threat of a general strike.

It was good tactics as well for the workers to concentrated on one issue—the demand for independent trade unions, which were perceived as the sole guarantee that the government would honor future promises to the workers and attend to future demands of the workers. The workers were not distracted on the one hand by immediate economic demands or on the other by broad political demands that would be explosive in their implications.

The existence of an independent Church in Poland lent enormous moral support to the workers' activities. Nonetheless, during the strikes and especially at the beginning, the Church hierarchy, and Cardinal Wyszynski in particular, played a rather ambiguous role. The Church clearly supported the workers, but just as clearly it feared that the workers' demands might go too far. It therefore sought to exert a moderating influence. Without any doubt, the workers and their spokesmen played the leading role in events. The Church found itself in the position of saying: "I am your leader, so I will follow you."

In the critical days of late summer and fall, the Party found itself in disarray. Its leader, Gierek, was ousted, and the new leader, Stanislaw Kania, had no time to establish a firm command. The Party activists and regional Party bureaucrats became, and remain, disoriented. The new unions exploited the resulting power vacuum in the political system.

Another absolutely crucial element in the vacuum was the position of the armed forces, which maintained neutrality on the issues. Moreover, it is reliably reported that as the crisis ripened the commander of the Polish armed forces, General Jaruzelski, informed the Party leaders at a crucial meeting of the Central Committee that the Polish Army could not be relied upon to intervene and eject workers forcibly from the occupied factories. This statement was a turning point, for it left the Party little choice but to negotiate seriously with the workers and to consent to major concessions. Threatened with a general strike and a complete breakdown of order, the new Polish regime accepted the workers' basic demands. This decision resulted not only from fear of workers' reaction to a rejection of their demands, but also from the fear that continued chaos in Poland and a general strike would increase the danger of Soviet intervention. At that point, the Polish leaders feared this outcome more than the workers did. . . .

But will the independent trade unions survive? The answer if of course a resounding "no" should the Soviets intervene directly in Poland. Even without intervention, however, can the victorious Polish workers translate paper agreements into actuality? This depends on two crucial elements: the behavior of the workers themselves and the situation within the Communist Party.

When speaking about the Party, it is essential to distinguish Poland in 1980 from Hungary in 1956 and Czechoslovakia in 1968. The Hungarian leadership under Imre Nagy and the Czech leadership under Dubĉek represented renegade Communist Parties which had adopted unorthodox and highly reformist positions that questioned the very political system and the alliance with the Soviet Union. The new Polish leadership under Kania cannot be characterized as renegade, even by the most generous imagination. Although far from homogeneous, it is composed basically of *politically* conservative communists who at the same time acknowledge the need for reforms, particularly in the areas of the economy and relations between Party and workers. Some leaders are more conservative and some more reformist; none, to our knowledge, questions the need to preserve the Party's monopoly, the need to enforce a policy of censorship, however revised, or, most of all, the need to maintain a close alliance with the Soviet Union.

As we have noted, this new leadership has yet to consolidate its power over a Party that remains disoriented and disorganized, especially at the provincial level. Factional struggle persists between hard-line and more moderate elements. Once consolidation comes about, however, there can be little doubt as to the tactics of the Party. It will aim to erode the workers' achievements, to wear down the workers, and to provoke continual skirmishes over specific items of contention. It will attempt to divide the workers, to isolate them from the dissident intellectuals, and to co-opt their leaders. It will also seek to define the lines of resistance to demands concerning political issues that patently involve the symbols and reality of communist rule in Poland, such as censorship and the security apparatus. At the same time, however, it will agree to compromise on immediate economic issues and on issues of structural economic reform. In other words, it will aim to preserve the essential non-negotiable characteristics of the system while being flexible on important but marginal elements of the system.

It is impossible now to say how successful these tactics will be. There is a strong likelihood that many of the workers' gains will survive even after the Party regroups and consolidates its power. Soviet intimidation and the fear of invasion act here as powerful weapons to moderate the workers' demands and to confine them within bounds that do not threaten to destroy the communist system itself. . . .

Poland requires far-reaching economic reforms to create a viable economy, to sustain steady increases in the standard of living, and to persuade Western creditors of the country's solvency. It needs a major change in agricultural policy, which would entail a redirection of large investments into the agrarian sector, a cancelling of restrictions on the growth of private farms, an extension of credits to farmers, and a restructuring of farm prices. It also needs reforms in the service sector. A policy like the Soviet New Economic Policy of 1921 should be introduced, encouraging craftsmen, artisans and small private entrepreneurs, and the prohibitive level of taxation on their activity should be abolished. But of greatest importance and difficulty, Poland requires a basic reform of the industrial system of planning, management and incentives—a reform that would resemble, or even go beyond, the

Hungarian model. Without such reforms, designed to cut drastically the waste in the Polish economy and to increase its productivity, any hopes for a long-range recovery of the economy are pipe dreams.

But here is the dilemma. Difficult and costly reforms such as these would require a transitional period of several years of austerity and self-denial for the consumer. In the long term, they would benefit the workers. In the short term, they would demand sacrifices. At present the workers, having lost their trust in government, see no incentive to accept these sacrifices. Only if more goods can be produced to satisfy the workers' needs will the government be able to gain their trust; yet such production increases themselves presuppose basic reforms.

Aside from promises, the government has only one recourse for breaking this vicious circle. It must meet the demands of workers for a role in running the factories and mines, and ultimately for a partnership in determining Polish economic policies. One may presume that the wisest Polish leaders understand that the workers' demands have to be met at least halfway. The key question here is whether such a governmental policy would be acceptable to Poland's communist neighbors, particularly the Soviet Union.

The events in Poland have very serious implications indeed for Poland's neighbors, for the Eastern bloc as a whole, and for the Soviet Union itself. To appreciate the depth of their concern one has only to survey the vicious attacks and warnings published in bloc countries, particularly East Germany and Czechoslovakia; the statements of Party leaders in those countries; and the increasingly hostile and frequent commentaries in the Soviet press. The reasons for the anxiety are clear: the economic, political and social issues that propelled the rise of a powerful workers' movement for reform in Poland are not absent in the other Eastern Bloc countries. Although the issues are more muted in these countries and the probability of their sparking a similar outburst is less immediate, victory for the Polish workers and the institutionalization of the role of independent unions as a counterweight to the monopoly of the Communist party could become a highly attractive example to workers in the rest of Eastern Europe.

Nor is the Soviet Union itself immune to labor unrest and the dangerous implications of raised workers' aspirations. Politically and economically, the decade of the 1980s will be a very harsh one for the Soviet Union. The extensive development that fueled Soviet economic advances over six decades can no longer assure the high growth rates of the past. Even if no other negative factors intervene and traditional Soviet economic management undergoes no decline in quality, the Gross National Product (GNP) will grow during the 1980s by only about 2.5 percent per year. The Soviet political-economic system of management, pricing and incentives is ill-prepared to maximize the possibilities for intensive growth. A relatively rapid shift to intensive growth would require fundamental changes in the political-economic system that are unlikely to be accomplished in the foreseeable future. Unfavorable demographic trends will exacerbate the situation. Not only will there be a rapid decline in the growth of new labor resources, but the increment to the labor forces will be overwhelmingly non-Russian in origin.

The Soviet energy balance will not favor economic growth, especially with regard to the production of oil. Economists concur in anticipating a decline, even if they dispute its extend. The decline will be sufficient, it seems, to impose major constraints on the Soviet economy and to limit Soviet ability to utilize fully their existing economic capacities.

With regard to agriculture, investments of the Brezhnev era have produced limited and, at best, uncertain results. This sector of the economy will remain highly volatile in the 1980s. Moreover, owing to the decline of long-term growth in other sectors, the unavoidable agricultural fluctuations will have a growing influence on the size of the Soviet GNP.

Just how difficult the Soviet economic situation will be in the 1980s is a matter of conjecture. According to the most pessimistic estimates, periods of low growth will alternate with downright economic stagnation. But even according to more optimistic estimates, the Soviet Union will experience economic pressures far more severe than anything it encountered during the 1960s and 1970s, when it was possible to have, simultaneously, high ratios of investment for economic growth, systematic and considerable increases in military spending, and steady though not always rapid increases in the standard of living of the Soviet people. Something will have to give. Taking into account the increasingly tense international situation and the growing Soviet energy demands, it seems most likely that redistribution of resources will adversely affect the consumer goods industries and lead to a decline in the rate of growth—or even stagnation—in the Soviet standard of living.

During the 1960s and 1970s, labor peace and social stability in the Soviet system were predicated to a large extent on the steady rise in consumption. It would be hardly accurate to speak of a revolution of rising expectations. As a matter of fact, the material expectations of the Soviet population, particularly its working class, are very modest and reasonable when compared to Western counterparts. Nevertheless, during the post-Stalin era the Soviet population, and expecially the working class, had learned to anticipate a continuous, if slow, rise in the standard of living. Neither we nor the Soviet leaders can predict how the working class will react to a protracted stagnation of consumption levels and continued shortages of food.

In my opinion, during the 1980s, the Soviet leaders will shift the focus of their concern and social policy. From the late 1920s to the early 1950s, Soviet social policy concentrated on achieving mastery and dominance over the peasantry. From the mid-1950s through the 1970s, the main concern was to neutralize the dissident movement and to achieve mastery over the growing professional classes in the Soviet Union—the technocrat, the economist, the expert. During the 1980s, the Party's principal aim will most likely be to extend its mastery over the industrial working class in order to assure labor peace. If so, the institutionalization of workers' power in Poland represents for the Soviet leadership a fearsome possibility, a dangerous and potentially infectious example. One suspects that the specter of "Polonization" hovers in the thoughts of Soviet leaders and elites.

Given these circumstances, Soviet leaders must consider the prospect of using force to change the course of Polish events. Yet it must be clear to them that the direct and indirect costs of invasion would be truly awesome, incomparably greater than those paid for the invasion of Hungary in 1956 and the invasion of Czechoslovakia in 1968.

First, in all probability an invasion of Poland would lead to a virtual state of war with the Polish workers and the Polish nation. While it is highly unlikely that the Polish armed forces would stand united against the invaders, it is very probable that individual major units would resist. All in all the exercise might become a very bloody and protracted affair. Such a military operation in the heart of a divided Europe could prove unpredictable and risky even in its military consequences. The behavior of other Warsaw Pact countries and armies cannot be surely predicted.

Second, the Soviet Union would acquire a staggering burden following the inevitable subjugation of the Polish nation. The Soviet government would not only have to maintain its occupying army, but would have to deliver extensive support to a nation of 35 million people. It would have to feed them, sustain their economy, and service their debt of $22 billion to the West. The Soviet economy could ill afford the strain, given the extent of Soviet domestic difficulties.

Third, an invasion of Poland and the possibility of an attendant massacre of Polish workers will almost certainly shatter the last ties between the Soviet Communist Party and the leading Communist Parties in Western Europe. In all probability the break between the Italian and Spanish Parties and Moscow would become final, and the intensity of their conflict with Moscow would rival that between the Soviet Union and China.

Fourth, an invasion of Poland would destroy one of the foundations, perhaps the cornerstone, of Soviet foreign policy since Afghanistan—the political, cultural and especially economic détente with Western Europe which survived the dissolution of détente with the United States. The Soviet Union has succeeded to a great extent in driving a wedge between the Western allies, separating its détente with Europe from its relations with the United States. This policy holds great political promise for the Soviet Union. It is also an economic necessity. A bloody invasion of Poland would shock both Left and Right in Europe and unite them in condemning the Soviets. It would probably go far to heal the ailing Western alliance and reverse for some time to come the advantages to the Soviet Union of détente with Europe.

Nowhere are the potential repercussions of invasion so serious for the Soviet Union as in the military area. The major case in point concerns the question of Theater Nuclear Forces in Europe. The significant divergence between Western European countries and the United States on TNF constitutes a principal source of disruption within the Western alliance. The United States, and especially the incoming Reagan Administration, regards the deployment of TNF in Europe as a first priority and a factor that will strengthen the Western bargaining position in negotiations with the Soviet Union. The Western European countries regard progress in negotiations on arms control with the Soviet Union as their first priority and the very precondition for the introduction of TNF into Europe. They have tied their consent for the deployment of TNF specifically to ratification of SALT II. This West European position on TNF afforded some consolation to the Soviet Union when SALT II was not ratified. A Soviet invasion of Poland would most probably alter the West European governments' policy in favor of the introduction of TNF without SALT II.

Fifth, invasion of Poland at a time when the new Reagan Administration is beginning to define its global policies would ensure a choice of direction most injurious to Soviet interests. It would reinforce the tendency to stress military buildup over arms control, to intensify the strategic rearmament of America and the deployment of TNF, to expand the capabilities of the Rapid Deployment Force, and to accelerate the search for U.S. bases in the Persian Gulf. It would also step up the momentum toward closer American-Chinese relations set underway during the last year of the Carter Administration and which now appears to face a less certain future, at least during the early part of the Reagan Administration. The invasion of Poland would doubtless create such revulsion in the United States that the anti-Soviet mood that helped Reagan into office would intensify significantly and facilitate the passage of military programs.

Finally, an invasion of Poland would surely affect the scale and nature of the Soviet military threat to NATO. It is quite possible, for example, that close to one million Soviet troops might be used for the invasion, and that a large part of these, say 300,000, would remain in Poland as an occupation force. In the short run this might mean some thinning of the 22 Soviet divisions in East Germany that now form the spearhead of the Soviet military posture directed against NATO. But the overwhelming likelihood is that the Soviets would call up or retain reserves to make up the difference rapidly, and the very state of mind revealed in a decision to invade could hardly be reassuring to the members of NATO. So there should certainly be no reason to let up in NATO's present increased defense program but on the contrary every reason to reaffirm and carry through that program, and possibly to increase the number and readiness of troops stationed in the Federal Republic of Germany.

It is thus clear that calculations of the direct and indirect, short-range and long-range consequences and implications of the invasion of Poland make such intervention the Soviet leadership's most difficult foreign policy decision in the post-Stalin era. This is why I believe that the threshold of Soviet tolerance for developments in Poland will be relatively high. An invasion would occur only in extreme circumstances and only after Soviet leadership had decided that the situation in Poland could not be salvaged by any other means.

As of mid-January 1981 the Soviet leadership still has reason to think that an accommodation can be reached between the Polish government and the workers whereby the workers will consent to de-escalate their demands. The Soviet leadership still has reason to hope that both the erosion of the workers' will and unity and the consolidation of the Polish communist leadership can be achieved through a series of measures such as co-optation, compromise, intimidation and the *threat* of invasion. Yet there remain at least three situations in which a Soviet invasion would be virtually unavoidable.

According to the first such scenario, demands of the workers escalate, the Polish government resists those demands, the workers call for strikes and possibly a general strike, the workers and students take to the streets, and the Polish government cannot use its own army and loses control of the situation.

According to the second scenario, the Polish government's resistance erodes under the pressure of workers' demands and the workers gradually attain virtual control of the factories and veto power over governmental policies.

According to the third scenario, a transformation takes place within the top echelons of the Communist Party and the Party embraces the demands of society: that is, a situation like that of Czechoslovakia in 1968.

How can these three situations be avoided? In my view the principal hope rests with the Polish Catholic Church. The Church looks upon an invasion of Poland as a threat to the physical survival of the Polish nation. It has not played a key role in recent Polish events, but has remained on the sidelines, extending moral support to the workers, for the most part observing and waiting. But toward the end of 1980 the Church did attempt to influence the contending Polish forces in the direction of moderation. If, in 1981, the unrest continues and workers' demands and the spontaneity of their expression increase, or if opposition to compromise should predominate within the government and Party leadership—either of which would surely enhance the chances of Soviet invasion—then the Church would probably bring the full weight of its authority to bear. A Church appeal to government and workers for moderation in the name of the national interest and unity would in all probability be heeded by both sides in Poland, and their response would gain precious time to attain at least a partial stabilization of the situation and to delay or forestall a Soviet decision to intervene.

One other institution in Poland might contribute to forestalling an invasion: the Polish armed forces. The Polish Army is a professional one. It accepts the primacy of the Party and is not normally involved in politics. In the present abnormal situation, however, its role in the political process has apparently increased, and its influence among the population has grown, thanks to its neutrality in recent months. An important December statement of the Polish Military Council concerning the dangers before Poland was, in fact, an appeal for calm in the struggle between workers and Party. At the same time it represented an assurance to the Soviet Union that should the government fail to cope with disorder, the Polish Army would this time be willing and ready to quell disturbances in an effort to prevent an invasion. Whether the Army can act effectively, however, depends decisively on the scale of unrest. An army composed largely of conscripts from the peasantry and working class cannot be used reliably to quell massive disorders supported by a majority of workers organized in the "Solidarity" union. The Army can be effective only in combatting and neutralizing regional disorders, against which reliable elite units can be used.

The United States and its Western allies can do very little to prevent a Soviet invasion of Poland. In the short term, they can also do very little to influence the situation inside Poland, except for extending humanitarian aid and credit as they have done during the autumn emergency. But should an invasion not take place, in the long term the United States and West European countries can significantly contribute to the constructive evolution of Polish development.

The economic question is crucial here, given what the Poles need and what we can offer. The governments of the United States and Western Europe, however, should not pursue a policy of extending credits without limits and conditions, for that would be throwing money into a bottomless barrel.

In my opinion, the proper policy for the United States is to act through a consortium formed with the West European states and especially the Federal Republic of Germany. This consortium would extend to Poland a graduated line of credit and aid in the amount of several billion dollars over the next four to five years, tied to a policy of serious economic reform by the Polish government. There should be a tacit understanding between the Poles and the consortium that particular installments of credit and aid would be forthcoming only to the extent that the Polish government proceeds step by step and quite rapidly to restructure its economic policies and system. It is in the best interests of the United States and Western Europe to ensure that the Polish experiment works. The policy proposed here would provide significant incentives to make it work.

It is extremely difficult to imagine a peaceful solution to the Polish events and a peaceful transformation of the Polish system that would allow greater freedom for society while preserving the political monopoly of the Communist Party. Everybody in Poland—worker, intellectual and Party member—knows that radical changes in the system are needed if Poland is to avoid economic and political bankruptcy. But at the same time, everybody knows, or is learning, that such radical changes are highly unlikely and may even be impossible owing to the Soviet military veto. This gap between the necessary and the possible is the reality of the Polish situation, and the measure of the gravity of the crisis.

We do not know whether the Soviets have decided to intervene in Poland. There are a number of options open to them short of full-scale invasion. There is the option they have already selected—to mass troops along Polish borders as a means of intimidating the workers and strengthening the backbone of the Polish leadership in resisting the workers' demands. The effectiveness and workability of this option will decline with time, however.

A second option involves the measured escalation of pressure by conducting military maneuvers on Polish soil. This action will push the Polish leaders to intensify their intimidation of the workers' movement. A third option would be most advantageous to the Soviet Union but highly doubtful in its effectiveness: Soviet troops would watch at the Polish border while the Polish Army and security forces themselves attempted to settle the situation.

A Soviet invasion of Poland would signal that Soviet leaders regard the workers' gains as irrevocable and the Polish Party throughly compromised by its vacillation and conciliatory attitude. It would signal that leaders in the Soviet Union and other East European communist states, particularly East Germany and Czechoslovakia, regard the existence of independent trade unions with even limited powers as incompatible with the concept of a communist state.

But a Soviet invasion of Poland would signal even more. It would tell us how much the Soviets fear their own working class, how much they fear for the stability of their East European empire. It would tell us that these fears are so profound that in the last analysis the Soviet Union is prepared to accept substantial and even irreversible losses in the international arena. Only a government that seriously doubts its own stability and that of its client states would deny the loyal communist leadership of Poland the time and latitude to manage its domestic problems. A leadership that is so insecure in its own country and empire presents grave dangers for states outside its sphere of influence, dangers magnified by the vast military power at its disposal. It will be extremely difficult to reach agreements with such a leadership, that is apprehensive as well as arrogant, on the regulation of competition in a turbulent world.

POLAND AND THE GHOST OF YALTA[2]

A specter again haunts Europe. Not the specter of communism, as Marx and Engels once wrote, for Soviet-style communism is scorned and discredited throughout the continent. It is the specter of Yalta that dominates European politics today, the specter of the unresolved legacy of World War II. For years it has lain dormant. Now it has been focused and dramatized by the events in Poland.

Ever since 1945, the Poles, like the other peoples of Eastern Europe, have been saddled with a government they did not choose through free elections. The fact that free elections were rarely held throughout much of that area, outside of Czechoslovakia, does not mitigate the indignity of their situation.

In addition to being unrepresentative, the Polish government also happens to be—unlike, for example, the Communist government of Hungary—grossly corrupt and incompetent. It is not surprising that the Polish people should want something better. Their efforts to improve the quality of their lives, to participate in decisions made in their name, and to break the hold of an autocratic dictatorship have won the admiration of people everywhere.

In a bureaucratized world, Solidarity, with its touches of syndicalism and even anarchism, seemed a triumph of the people over the state. Even governments that abhor and would forcibly put down such actions within their own frontiers have publicly praised the Polish workers' movement. Such governmental praise,

[2]Reprint of an article by Ronald Steel, author of *Walter Lippman and the American Century, Pax Americana* and *The End of Alliance,* and numerous articles on foreign affairs. *New Republic.* 186:13–5. Ja. 27, '82. Reprinted by permission of THE NEW REPUBLIC. Copyright © 1982 by The New Republic, Inc.

however, is largely for reasons of state rather than for reasons of the heart.

What makes the Polish case different is not only that the Poles wanted to be free to elect their own government—an inalienable right all too often alienated in the world today and, for that matter, Polish history—but also to throw off the Soviet yoke. The Russians run a nasty empire kept together only by military occupation and the fear of force. In their effort to shed Soviet imperialism and the incompetence of their own Communist rulers, the Poles deserve our admiration and, insofar as possible, our support.

But there are sharp limitations on the kind of support we can offer. The decision by the Polish military—in conjunction with the discredited Communist Party and the Russians—to suppress the Solidarity movement has dramatized certain ambiguities. One is the fact that Polish recruits have remained loyal to their offices, even when it meant turning against factory workers very much like themselves. Another is that the one thing the Reagan Administration was expecting, and which some members of the Administration seemed almost to welcome, has not happened—that is, a Soviet invasion. The Russians so far have managed to keep this an essentially Polish matter, no matter how much they may have orchestrated it.

It is easy enough for American officials and editorial writers to berate the Europeans for not breaking trade relations with Moscow. It might be less easy if American workers were as dependent for their jobs on Communist markets as are West European workers. It might also be easier if the Administration were able either to demonstrate that sanctions will work or to be less hypocritical in its actions. Its refusal to send food to Warsaw while selling wheat to Moscow—as columnist Mary McGrory put it, feeding the Russians while starving the Poles—seems inspired by something other than high principle.

What is happening in Poland is sad; it is unfair; it is outrageous. We have every right to denounce it. Not because our own hands are totally clean—for they certainly are not, in places like El Salvador and Chile—but in the name of an offended human decency and dignity. We should speak up against oppression wherever it occurs and whoever commits it, holding up the same standards to ourselves that we do to others.

The Polish drama—one of an aroused people against the power of an oppressive state apparatus—would be inspiring wherever it took place. It is complicated in this case, as Polish matters usually are, by geography and cold war politics. Poland's position between Germany and Russia has traditionally made it an area of contention. What happens in Poland inevitably sucks in the major powers that flank her. The Polish question has historically been a European one. Now it is an international question as well.

The other complication, of course, is the struggle between communism and Western liberalism, between Russia and the West. Poland represents not only a breakdown of the Communist economic system, but a failure of Russia's ability to control events within its own empire. To be sure, "order" of a sort is being restored in Poland. But modern societies cannot function for long under bayonets and martial law. Nor can an empire be held together in this manner. The Polish uprising is another stage in the gradual decay of Moscow's East European empire.

The question is not whether such decay is taking place, but the manner in which it shall be managed and the dangers that any sudden upheaval might pose. Great powers do not normally treat with equanimity the collapse of their empires, particularly when it takes place on their frontiers. It is one thing for the Russians to lose countries like Egypt and Somalia overnight when third world leaders ungratefully decide to switch benefactors. It is something else to lose Poland, the thoroughfare for so many invasions from the West, two of them within the memory of most Russians.

Thus the drama taking place in Poland is not simply one of the good guys against the bad, of Solidarity against an autocratic and corrupt regime. And it is not just one that involves the Russians and the Poles. It is also a drama of diplomacy, international finance, spheres of influence, and balances of power. This is not an inspirational story. It is even a bit sordid. But it is unavoidable, for it involves the stability of the European state system and many of the institutions that govern the cold war world.

This is the reason why, although everyone sympathizes with the Solidarity movement, virtually no responsible Western official wanted it to take control of the Polish state. Not the bankers in Dusseldorf, London, and New York, who are holding some $27 billion in promissory notes from the Polish government. Not the Catholic Church, which long ago worked out an arrangement with Polish Communists and fears restrictions on its activities in Eastern Europe. Not foreign offices on both sides of the Iron Curtain, which have seen the advantages of ostpolitik and do not want to anger Moscow unnecessarily. Not officials of NATO and the Warsaw Pact, who have accommodated themselves to a Europe divided into manageable halves.

The simple truth is that there is not a lot that the West can do about Poland—other, perhaps, than financing an incompetently managed economy. And a further truth is that any radical political change in Poland would have incalculable consequences for the political balance in Europe.

Although Solidarity began by seeking relatively limited changes, the revolution—and a revolution it certainly was—developed a momentum of its own. No one knows where it would have stopped. Quite possibly with the destruction of the Communist Party's monopoly of power and even the withdrawal of Poland from the Warsaw Pact. This is one thing the Russians cannot now allow, so long as they are capable of preventing it. And no matter how much the West might welcome this emotionally, it also poses a great many dangers.

If the Soviets were able to prevent it by force, we would be back where we started, indeed, where we have been since 1945. If they were not able, then the liberation movement would almost certainly spread throughout Eastern Europe. Freedom, after all, is contagious. The Russians could lose control even of East Germany. The Iron Curtain could collapse.

In one sense that would be a wonderful day. The partition of Europe cannot and must not last forever. But with the Iron Curtain would also collapse virtually every innovative institution in the Western alliance: NATO, the Common Market, the Organization of Economic Cooperation and Development, even the Federal Republic of Germany. All are based on the cold war division of Europe.

That division was not caused by choice, but by necessity; initially by Hitler's aggression and then by the fact that the Soviet Union carried the brunt of the land war against Nazi Germany.

America and Britain desperately needed and encouraged the Russian military advance through Eastern Europe. They did not, of course, want them to stay after the war was over. But they also knew that there was little they could do about it. Moscow was determined to contain the power of Germany and never again to allow Eastern Europe to fall into hostile hands.

At the Yalta Conference in February 1945, FDR and Churchill agreed that the new government of Poland should be "friendly" to the Soviet Union, and won Stalin's agreement for "free and unfettered elections" in that country. The two objectives were incompatible. The elections were a mockery. The Russians established control over Poland and a few years later over the other East European countries they occupied. Although their sphere of influence was contested, it was never seriously challenged.

Since 1948, with the Czech coup, Europe has been divided. Each side recognizes the other's sphere of influence; each recognizes that any attempt to change it by force would mean war. Every Administration, Republican or Democratic, has honored that unofficial aggreement—not because they wanted to, but because there was no realistic alternative.

Henry Kissinger's deputy, the unfairly abused and misquoted Helmut Sonnenfeldt, pointed out in 1976 that although Eastern Europe is within the "scope and area of natural interest" of the Russians, it has been unable to acquire loyalty in the area other than through force of arms. It should be the objective of the West to transform that "inorganic, unnatural relationship," with its danger to world peace, into an "organic," or nonmilitary one. Our policy, he observed, should be one of "responding to the clearly visible aspirations in Eastern Europe for a more autonomous existence within the context of a strong Soviet geopolitical influence."

That is the heart of the so-called Sonnenfeldt Doctrine. Its observations are unexceptionable and have been operating policy for more than thirty years. They state what everybody knows: that peace in Europe hinges on political stability, and that the interests of both sides can be best served by each respecting the other's sphere of influence in Europe.

Like it or not, the division of Europe is, for the foreseeable future, a fact of life, one that reflects the interests of both superpowers. It cannot be resolved by force. Any dramatic change could wreck both alliance systems. If Poland suddenly pulled itself free from Russian control, the regime in East Germany would be isolated. Bonn, which has ignored the dream of reunification because it seemed so unattainable, might then be tempted to look East. What German political leader could afford to turn his back on the "lost territories" if there seemed a hypothetical chance of regaining them? Bonn's hard-forged links to NATO and the Common Market would be called into question. The ominous specter of a unified Reich would suddenly take form, bringing unknown dangers into European politics. With the German question reopened, all the institutions we have taken for granted would be called into question. NATO would in all likelihood collapse, and with it the major instrument for American control over Western Europe.

Although the division of Europe is an abomination, virtually any conceivable alternative poses enormous risks—not only to the rival alliance systems, but to the political balance that for the first time since 1914 has brought relative tranquility to the continent. This is why the governments of Europe have been restrained in their reaction to the imposition of martial law in Poland. It is also why the Reagan Administration, however much it enjoys Moscow's embarrassment, must recognize that a sudden disruption of the political balance in Europe could be detrimental to both superpowers.

The problem today remains the one laid out in the Sonnenfeldt memo: how to nurture greater political freedom in Eastern Europe in a way that will not suddenly disrupt the political balance, not reopen the German question, and not seem an intolerable threat to the Soviet Union. The problem is how to acknowledge Russia's obvious geopolitical influence in the area while working toward a more "organic" relationship that does not rest on fear, force, and intimidation.

The events in Poland have shown that the Soviet empire is not immutable. Change is eternal and unavoidable. But it comes at a price. That price will be paid on both sides of the Iron Curtain and on the institutions that are the products of Europe's partition. There is no indication that Washington, any more than Moscow, is prepared for such changes.

The harsh reality is that the superpowers have a vested interest in the status quo. Each enjoys rumbles of discontent within the other's empire; neither is willing to face the effect that an upheaval on the other side of the Iron Curtain might have on its own alliance system. Solidarity challenged the Soviet empire directly and the European status quo indirectly. The armed force that keeps the Warsaw Pact together is what provides the rationale for NATO. If we are to encourage the demise of the Warsaw Pact, we had better be prepared for profound shocks to our own alliance as well.

WHAT POLAND MEANS[3]

The first reaction to the military coup in Poland was shock and confusion, followed by a wave of indignation, anger, and protest. Protests are important, but they will lead nowhere unless an analysis is made of what went wrong and why. A defeat always contains lessons for the future. What are the lessons of the defeat in Poland?

According to the old U.S. cavalry manual, a commander might be excused for being defeated but never for being surprised. By this rule, almost everyone involved in the events in Poland stands condemned. The Polish counterrevolution of December 1981 was predictable, and yet it took the great majority of Poles unawares, just as it did most observers outside Poland.

It had always been assumed that an operation of the magnitude of the Polish coup, in which divisions were mobilized, and many hundreds of tanks and personnel carriers were moved from place to place, could not occur without some warning signs. But there were no warning signs, and this despite the fact that the operation was mounted not in the secrecy of Soviet military districts but in the semi-open society which Poland had become prior to December 1981.

[3]Reprint of an article by Walter Laqueur, Chairman of the Research Council of Georgetown University's Center for Strategic and International Studies and a contributing editor to *Commentary*. *Commentary*. 73:25–30. Mr. '82. Reprinted by permission of the author.

The genuine intelligence failure was not, of course, the technical one of failing to pick up the radio traffic from the Polish Army High Command and the secret police; it was the conviction that something like this simply could not happen.

Before December 1981, it had been widely believed that the achievements of the Polish October were irreversible. If there were to be an attempt to do away with them, nothing less than a full-scale Soviet invasion would suffice. This belief in the lasting gains of Solidarity was common to "hawks" and "doves." As both groups saw it, Solidarity had shown that gradual change in the Soviet empire was now possible. Thus Leszek Kolakowski: "The standard way in which Western politicians used to explain away their appeasement policy—'Nothing can change in the Soviet bloc unless it starts from Moscow'—becomes less and not more credible. In fact, there is nothing in the history of empires to prove that their disintegration process cannot be given impulse from peripheries—and this is what is happening right now."

The observation was not *a priori* false; the disintegration of empires has frequently begun on the periphery. But this did not mean that it was happening now to the Soviet empire. In fact, two hundred years of Polish history should have given Kolakowski and others pause: the Poles rebelled many times against their czarist oppressors but their uprisings had not the slightest impact on the Russian people. In 1981 a Polish independence movement might have prevailed, but only if the impulse had been coming from above, as it previously had in China and Yugoslavia, in Rumania and Albania. In other words, the movement might have succeeded if the key positions in state and party, in the army and the political police, had been in the hands of the rebels. This, of course, was not the case in Poland. While Solidarity had a great deal of moral support, it had no power.

Another reason for the misplaced optimism of many observers was the idea that the Polish game was, from the Soviet point of view, no longer worth the candle. True, the Soviet Union had legitimate security interests in Poland which it would not give up. But if the Poles behaved prudently, if they did not question the Soviet military presence, the Russians might be willing, in the end, to reconsider existing arrangements. Eventually, something like a Finlandized Poland might emerge, internally free, but part of the Soviet security system.

Shortly after the Jaruzelski coup, for example, George Kennan wrote: "Had Solidarity been willing to pause as recently as a month or two ago—to rest for a while on its laurels and to give time for Moscow to satisfy itself that freedom in Poland did not mean the immediate collapse of the heavens—it would already have had to its credit a historic achievement. . . . "

Yet there is no good reason to assume that the Soviet Union had ever been willing to put up with the gains of Solidarity—not with those of November 1981 and not with those of November 1980. This is something we know now from the new rulers of Poland themselves. The basic flaw in Kennan's argument goes further back—to the assumption common to all revisionist historiography (though not at the time to Kennan himself) that in 1946 Stalin did not really want to "Sovietize" Poland, that he only reluctantly moved in this direction after Truman had declared cold war on him. Obviously, if the Soviet Union had only reluctantly absorbed Poland in 1947, it might be willing to give it up in 1981.

But apart from the fact that the Sovietization of Eastern Europe was *not* undertaken reluctantly by Stalin, it was forgotten by Kennan and others that Brezhnev and his colleagues had made it clear, both in private conversations and in solemn declarations (notably the Brezhnev Doctrine), that they would never, if they could help it, let go of any territory occupied in 1944–45. If the Czars never voluntarily let go of Poland, why would Brezhnev and his colleagues, good Russian patriots, do any less? The idea that they would was based on a misreading of Russian history; in addition, it was based on a misreading of the character of the Soviet system. For as the Russians see it, "security" means not only territorial buffers but political ones as well. How then could they tolerate free trade unions in Poland and the political and cultural pluralism such unions imply?

That the coup came as a surprise in the West was due to a failure of intelligence, but that so many arguments were adduced in the West to justify the coup was due to gullibility. It is pointless to discuss these arguments in detail. They were mostly wrong, yet they were widely believed. One day historians will point to the indisputable fact that whenever a dictator has come to power in this century, there has been a widespread tendency to give him the benefit of the doubt, to look for mitigating circumstances; Mussolini is an interesting example. It is also true that some in the West felt relief when the news of the coup was received. Poland was the "headache of the West," as Roosevelt once called it in an unguarded moment, and General Jaruzelski had at last provided a cure.

All this may explain the Church-knows-best argument which was invoked at first as an excuse for doing nothing. The Church was indeed well-informed and it moved, in the beginning, with great, perhaps exaggerated, caution. But the Church always behaves more cautiously than sovereign states. Not only does it lack "divisions" in the form of political and economic clout; its main concern over the centuries has been to survive. When the Church, after a week or two, became more outspoken in its condemnation of the military regime, those who had used it as an alibi for inaction shifted their ground to a variety of other specious rationalizations.

Governments were about as confused as the media. There was silence not only from the European capitals but also so much caution and restrained statesmanship from Washington that the President and his chief aides received praise from unexpected quarters (like Anthony Lewis of the New York *Times*). In France, notwithstanding many brave words in the press, Foreign Minister Cheysson, when he was asked whether the French government had any intention of doing anything, answered, "Absolutely not." Ironically, the German *Bundestag* was the first Western parliament to pass a resolution critical of the Polish coup.

After about a week the Reagan administration and most of the American media became more outspoken. But there were also not a few voices still insisting that while events in Poland were unfortunate, because they endangered détente and provided fresh ammunition to the hawks, order in Poland had after all somehow to be restored. If the status quo in Europe were upset and the Soviet Union lost control over Poland, the results could well be disastrous. Moreover, a dialogue with the Soviet leaders was now even more urgent than before.

Sometimes these arguments were made by men of the Left, occasionally by right-wingers; in West Germany young Socialists and big bankers found themselves on the same side of the barricades.

All this confusion in the West was perhaps to be expected. After all, for most Americans and even for many Europeans, Poland was a faraway country of which they knew little. But why did the coup take so many Poles by surprise, and why was hardly any resistance offered?

Solidarity had developed almost overnight into a movement of many millions; like a mighty river, it seemed to sweep everything along with it. It was not a political party and there was no apparatus, but there was an enormous amount of enthusiasm and of the volunteer spirit. As every practitioner and student of politics knows, however, good will cannot possibly replace organization. Of course even a much stronger organization might not have helped. The mighty German trade unions collapsed like a house of cards in 1933 in the face of the Nazi onslaught; so did the Social Democratic party and even the Communists, who had an illegal apparatus and were, in theory at least, ready to operate underground. In general, democratic mass movements do not have much of a chance against modern dictatorships. Thus even a well-prepared Solidarity would probably have been defeated. But it was not prepared.

The possibility of a Soviet intervention had been discussed in the non-legal Polish press in 1980 and it had been assumed that this was likely only if Poland were to leave the Warsaw Pact or if the Communist party disintegrated altogether.

The leaders of Solidarity had no wish to provoke the Soviets and they thought, a little naively, that the Russians and the Polish Communist leadership were willing to accept the Solidarity concept of a new Poland; a division of power among the party, the free trade unions, and the Church. The working class of the West had compelled capitalism to make concessions, and the Poles believed that Communism too would make similar concessions under pressure. Intellectuals like Jacek Kuroń, who only a few years earlier refused to give any credence to the possibility of gradual change under Communism, had concluded by 1980 that such a chance existed and that the attempt should be made to enlarge the sphere of freedom within a totalitarian society. They accepted that Poland was not a sovereign country, that all important decisions were taken in Moscow, and that this was the root of all evil. But a cautious optimism had been growing since about 1976. Some improvement could be achieved.

What if the Russians invaded? This was held to be quite unlikely, partly because of Afghanistan. In any case, no special preparations were necessary since the Soviets would encounter popular resistance, just as the Germans had in World War II. The possibility of a coup from within was apparently not seriously considered, though it was thought that there would be constant Soviet pressure on the Polish leadership to take a much tougher line. Thus, no one was prepared when the army struck on December 13, and in the very first hours of the state of siege almost the entire leadership of the opposition was arrested.

Solidarity overrated its own strength and gravely underrated the power of its adversaries. The union had flourished during the eighteen months before December 1981 because the Communist party was so demoralized that it had virtually ceased to exist as a force capable of running the country. But there were other forces waiting in the wings to fill the power vacuum: the hard core of party diehards, the secret police, and the army.

Solidarity (and most foreign observers) had tended to ignore or discount these forces: how could they possibly prevail over the great majority of their fellow citizens? The army was, after all, a people's army. Most of the soldiers were recruits—flesh of the flesh of the working class and of the peasantry. Surely, they would not shoot at fellow Poles: Jaruzelski himself said so. In any event, secret policemen could not milk cows, nor could tanks do the work in factories. The counterrevolutionaries knew it and for this reason, *la mort dans l'âme,* they would not even try.

These arguments underestimated the number of potential collaborators of the counterrevolutionary party, and they exaggerated the difficulties involved in destroying a popular movement and holding the population at bay, at least in the short run. There was a substantial array of collaborators: the 150,000 regular army officers and sergeants, along with 100,000 internal-security forces and other police agents and paramilitary troops who had been indoctrinated over the years and kept in isolation from the masses. These people had not been infected by the democratic virus; on the contrary, they had become even more firmly resolved to "put an end to anarchy."

In addition, there was in Poland (as in every East European country) a sizable stratum of people who had served the old order more or less faithfully, who by no means believed in the official ideology but who had become so identified with the status quo that they had to fight for it in a crisis—fight for their jobs, for their survival. Like the party diehards, they had nowhere to go; they rightly assumed that in a free Poland there was no room for yesterday's bosses, censors, propagandists, gendarmes, and torturers.

There were quite a few of these, and their ranks were swelled by thousands of others—the *spostati*, the flotsam-and-jetsam of all social groups, disappointed officials who now saw a chance for rapid promotion, *lumpen* intellectuals who resented their more gifted colleagues, the eternally discontented, the opportunists of every kind ready to throw in their lot with the likely victor, criminal and semi-criminal elements—the scum found at the margins of every society: all far more numerous than is usually believed.

It does not follow from all this that the Polish freedom movement was doomed from the very beginning and that the members of Solidarity were mistaken in launching their struggle in the first place. Unless some courageous people are willing to risk their freedom and even their lives, no tyranny can ever be broken. Kuron was right when he wrote in his "Program for a New Poland" (1977) that successful resistance was possible in a totalitarian system. But he failed to see that the very success of the opposition was its undoing. The ruling group could afford only those concessions which would not endanger its hold; beyond this the totalitarian regime could not go, short of committing suicide. If Solidarity had won over the army command, it might have been able to resist Soviet pressure, but this was impossible. Thus one is back to the starting point: the only successful revolutions in the Communist bloc are those carried out from above, not from below, and the revolutions from above are not usually democratic in character.

Organizationally, the December coup was an outstanding success. The preparations went on for many months, and must have involved hundreds, if not thousands, of people. Yet the leaders of Solidarity, who were so sure that little that happened in Poland would escape them, had not the faintest inkling. The details of the preparation of the coup are as yet unknown, but it seems highly likely that the initiative came from the Soviet Politburo which had given up hope that the Polish party was capable of suppressing Solidarity, and that the task was assigned by the KGB to the Polish secret police and a small group of trusted Polish leaders like Olszowski and Jaruzelski.

Although the Kremlin does not like political soldiers, who may develop an appetite for power and even independence (faithful Stalinists like Mao, Tito, and Enver Hoxha developed just such an appetite after donning military uniforms), a military coup was from the point of view of the Soviets the best possible solution. Certainly it was far better for the Russians than having to do the job themselves. A direct Soviet invasion would have entailed much greater political costs in relations with the West. And whereas the Poles might resist Russian troops, it was thought that they would be most reluctant to resist their own officers and soldiers.

It was also relatively easy to equip the generals with an ideology of sorts. The main element was nationalism with the stress on collaboration for geopolitical reasons with the Soviet Union. Secondly, populism—attacks on the "rich" and "corrupt" from the relatively liberal Gierek era, against intellectuals (most of whom are by definition suspect), Jews, freemasons, and so on. As for the Church, it was to be treated gently, at least in the early stage; its turn would come later on, for its power would have to be broken to prevent a recurrence of the events of 1980–81.

The pseudo-Jacobinism of the fight against corruption is, of course, fraudulent: the present leaders have committed the same abuses as those who now find themselves in the dock. But the basis of the new regime is not really to be sought in the ideological sphere; it is a matter of naked power. Once, Communism stood for the political mobilization of the masses; today the aim is de-politicization by atomizing society, by trying to incite workers against intellectuals and against peasants, by providing entertainment from football to alcohol (the rulers may not be able to provide *panem* but they can still offer *circenses*), and by creating the impression that the new regime is omnipresent and resistance therefore hopeless.

Just as Solidarity and many of its well-wishers abroad underestimated the strength of the forces ranged against it, so they underrated the power and effectiveness of even a moderately modern dictatorship. Even the discredited czarist regime dominated Poland without much difficulty; but for the Russian collapse of 1917, there would have been no independent Poland. Supervision and political control in modern societies is far easier yet. A hundred years ago, a terrorist who wanted to plunge a town into darkness had to go from house to house and smash every single lamp. A contemporary terrorist merely has to blow out a fuse in the central energy supply plant to achieve his aim. What is true for terrorism from below is equally true for terrorism from above. The counterrevolution simply disconnected the telephones and banned intercity travel, thereby putting Solidarity back to 1863, whereas the junta still had at its disposal all the modern means of communication.

What of the future? The army, it has been said, may destroy free unions, but how will it make the peasants and the workers work? On this point too the difficulties are exaggerated. The present situation in Poland is certainly not conducive to establishing production records. But it is also true that the majority of the population will go on following its daily pursuits. Poles do not want to starve and they will do at least a necessary minimum of work. Passive resistance in the fields and factories will not bring the government down.

One need not invoke visions of Fritz Lang's *Metropolis* or of Orwell, with armed police stationed in the factories, to conclude that the near-term outlook for Poland is grim. And not only for Poland: the economic barometer all over Eastern Europe indicates bad weather—even Czechoslovakia with its factories which resemble museums, even East Germany, even Hungary, the showcase of the Eastern bloc, are experiencing negative growth for the third year in a row.

Has, then, the return to a more repressive policy, a Stalinism without Stalin, become inevitable all over Eastern Europe? It is difficult to imagine that the Soviet leaders or their East European representatives actually want such a policy. It would be an admission of bankruptcy, and, worse yet, it would lead, as it did in the past, to purges and repression *inside* the ranks of the party. However, Communist leaders may not be able to think of any other way to maintain control. Some of them are quite willing to try far-reaching economic concessions deviating from the classic Leninist pattern of economic organization. But in present circumstances even sensible economic reforms would not produce results in the foreseeable future. Neo-Stalinism will not improve economic performance either, but it will at least suppress manifestations of discontent.

Nevertheless neo-Stalinism is likely to fail for other reasons. In the early postwar period, during the heyday of Sovietization in Eastern Europe, there was terror, but there was also idealism and enthusiasm, especially among the younger generation and the intellectuals. The sacrifices were deemed necessary to build a better tomorrow. Now that the harvest has been reaped, a repeat performance can no longer count on popular support. Furthermore, a working class has come into being far more educated and politically sophisticated than the workers of 1950, who frequently were only a little removed from the village.

Under these conditions, the only effective appeal is to nationalism. Yet in a period of genuine conflicts of interest (for instance, over the allocation of resources), nationalism in Eastern Europe is bound to be anti-Soviet in character. Moreover, there is bound to be conflict within the Communist leadership: the military and the secret police will demand representation commensurate with their real importance as pillars of the regime. Failures will generate friction between individuals and groups, scapegoats will be needed every little while. Poor Eastern Europe, even its dictators cannot be envied.

In all these ways, in short, the Soviet system is producing the internal contradictions which will eventually destroy it (as Marx ironically predicted would happen to the capitalist system). But it still remains true that repression may work for years to come.

The question then arises of what, in the meantime, the West can and should do.

It has been asked why so much fuss has been made about Poland. After all, it was clear from the beginning that nothing could be done to help the Poles anyway. Poland had become part of the Soviet sphere at Yalta and no force in the world could dislodge the Russians.

The argument that nothing can be done about Poland is a half-truth. That no one intends to launch a war over Poland in the nuclear age goes without saying; nor is there any way to restore full sovereignty to Poland. But it is also true that the Soviets (and the Polish neo-Stalinists) could be made to pay a high price, not to "punish" them but as a matter of Western self-preservation.

By all rules, the instigators and perpetrators of the Polish coup should be on the defensive, but instead of a crisis of the Soviet empire, we face a crisis of the Western alliance. The reason is the unwillingness to accept that support for Poland is not a moralistic-romantic gesture but a political necessity. To be sure, Poland is *also* a moral issue; it is, as Marx wrote to Engels in 1856, the "external thermometer," the yardstick by which the "courage and vitality" of political movements can be measured. Marx, whatever his faults, was not a naive man. He knew that the Czar would not lose much sleep because so many anti-Russian resolutions were passed in Poland or because of poems like "And Freedom Shrieked as Kosciuszko Fell." But he also knew that speaking out against the forces of depotism was as important for the West's own self-respect as for the Polish cause. The idea that states, in contrast to individuals, have "interests not sentiments" is true. But it is true only of declining nations—small in size and of little faith.

What then can be done about Poland? Above all, the facts have to be made known to the Eastern European nations and the peoples of the Soviet Union. Communist strategy in Eastern Europe is to deny political information to the population, to make it docile through ignorance and apathy. It is precisely in these circumstances that Western broadcasting services could play an enormous role.

Secondly, there is the issue of economic sanctions. The pro-Soviet-trade lobby in Washington has been arguing for a long time that all sanctions are ineffectual. In Europe the pro-Soviet trade lobby is afraid that sanctions are so effective that they will lead to war, and that the West on the contrary should be interested in enlarging its trade relations with the Soviet bloc, because a prosperous Soviet Union will be far more inclined to pursue a moderate policy at home and abroad.

Yet it is clearly beyond the capacity of the democracies to make the Soviet bloc a going economic concern, especially at the present time, when they themselves face difficulties at home. Even if it were possible, it is doubtful whether the political consequences would be as beneficial as we are told. It is more likely that a further influx of Western capital and know-how would be used for purposes detrimental to Western interests (as indeed has already been the case in connection with the Soviet military build-up). A Polish author, Stefan Kisiliewski, recently noted that many of those who advocate closer economic ties with the Soviet bloc could not care less about "moderation" in Poland (or elsewhere); they are interested in profits, not freedom. It is doubtful that the court of history will find Kisiliewski guilty of libel.

To be sure, there is some weight to the argument that sanctions do not work. Sanctions have worked against small countries or those lacking some essential raw materials. A very big economy like Comecon (the combined economies of the Soviet bloc) is much less vulnerable. For this reason, interference with normal trade relations is unlikely to have decisive political effects.

On the other hand, economic sanctions do have a certain impact in certain conditions. Even the post-Afghanistan grain embargo, which President Reagan called "ineffective," hurt the Soviet Union: the Russians got less grain than they wanted and they had to pay at least a billion dollars more for what they got.

A grain embargo over a prolonged period would certainly affect the Soviet economy and would perhaps even compel the Soviet leaders to cut down defense spending. But such a step would probably have to involve compensation for U.S. farmers (even though they have been doing very well in other parts of the world—1980 and 1981 were record years). It would also involve a major political effort to influence Argentina, Canada, and Australia to follow the U.S. example, or at least to reduce their exports drastically.

Whether the Reagan administration is willing to make the effort is another question.

Even more serious is the issue of credits. Western bankers have been pouring billions into the Comecon economies. They were told by their political advisers that there was really no risk since the East European system was very stable and if the worst came to the worst there was always the "Soviet umbrella." They were not told that East Europe had become a drain on Soviet resources for the last fifteen years and that Western bankers, through their massive credits, were helping the Soviet Union to maintain its empire. One could take a more detached view of these harebrained credits if the damage were limited to those responsible. In actual fact, Western taxpayers, directly or indirectly, will have to foot the bill—not to mention the political costs.

Today *all* East European countries (including East Germany and Hungary) face major financial difficulties. Poland alone will need about $20 billion during the next few years; by 1985 the Comecon hard-currency debt will have risen (according to the Wharton forecast) to $125–140 billion. Poland is already unable to repay the principal and interest on its debt; other Comecon countries will reach this stage within a year or two. Yet the Soviet umbrella is nowhere to be seen. Soviet economic planners apparently assume that the Western banks now have such a heavy stake in Poland and other Comecon countries that they cannot allow them to collapse.

Lenin's famous dictum about foreign capitalists being willing to do almost anything for profit, including supply the rope for their own hanging, is thus being taken one step further: now that there is no profit anymore and Comecon cannot afford even to pay for the rope, Western capitalists are evidently ready to *give* them the money with which to buy it. John Barry, an economic commentator, has noted that Italy was shut out of the Euromarket (i.e., forbidden further loans) when its debt-service ratio reached 10 percent; in the case of Eastern Europe, Western bankers went on lending even when the ratio reached 25 percent or even more. True, they shut out Poland from the medium- and long-term credit market when Solidarity appeared on the scene. Should they give General Jaruzelski what they refused to Lech Walesa?

Some say yes. They argue that unless the West pursues a more positive policy combining carrot with stick, it will have no influence whatsoever on events in Poland. Therefore it should express its willingness to reschedule the loans on condition that General Jaruzelski and the Communists reach a new "social contract" with the Polish people. The sentiments are as praiseworthy as the idea is foolish. For if such a social contract were possible there would have been no need for the military takeover in the first place.

Since the Soviet Union dominates Eastern Europe, there is no sound reason why it should not be forced to accept full financial responsibility for the policies pursued under its aegis. If it is unwilling to do so, these economies should be allowed to collapse. Yet some of the banks are by now captives of their own mistakes and they are willing to pour good money after bad if only to postpone the inevitable day of reckoning.

There remain two further issues—the "export" of high technology via various "fronts" in Europe, and the Soviet-European gas pipeline. The former ranges from initial-guidance technology and high-energy laser mirrors to state-of-the-art computers and software technology. The illegal transfer or theft of such technology has been a major scandal; it is a matter for the FBI rather than the Secretary of Commerce to deal with. As for the gas pipeline, it is a European rather than an American problem, though of course it affects the future of the alliance. For those in Europe who even today behave as if they no longer have full freedom of action will certainly show even greater caution once their dependence on Soviet supplies increases. An overall Western energy policy could do much to reduce Europe's vulnerability, but there has been no advance at all in this direction for years. On the other hand, some European industries at present in difficulties hope that the natural-gas deal will provide work for a number of years. It is a short-sighted approach, since the deal will not solve any basic problems and will only postpone hard decisions.

If peaceful, gradual change in the Soviet empire were possible, it would certainly be in the interests of the West to assist in the process. But the main lesson of Poland seems to be that only through violent spasms will significant change occur. In view of this reality, Western gifts to the Soviet bloc are contrary not only to the interests of the West but to the interests of the people of Eastern Europe as well.

CLASH OVER POLAND[4]

Although martial law in Poland came as a strong blow to American public opinion, it was not entirely unexpected. For many months authorities in Washington warned that a crackdown might occur. But precisely because the alarms were so numerous and so frequently premature, hope gradually developed in the United States that the Polish experiment would be allowed to run its course.

Frustration and indignation with General Wojciech Jaruzelski's coup are understandable and indeed justifiable. But emotional outrage rarely amounts to a coherent and effective foreign policy. Practitioners of geopolitics, like surgeons, are judged not by their sympathy with a patient's suffering but by their ability to help the victim combat the disease. Both encounter tragedy daily, whether they must amputate cancer-stricken limbs or deal with distasteful and brutal regimes. Unlike surgeons, however, architects of foreign policy must constantly reconcile many conflicting interests: The well-being of the patient, or of any friend or ally, is merely one of them.

The Reagan administration's response to the Polish crisis should be evaluated against this background. Some influential critics of U.S. policy since the introduction of martial law in Poland have charged that Washington has not done enough to pressure the military authorities in Warsaw and their sponsors in Moscow to stop their offensive against Poland's independent trade-union movement, Solidarity. It would be gratifying if the United States had the power to help the Polish workers. But oppo-

    [4]Reprint of an article by Dimitri K. Simes, Executive Director of the Soviet and Eastern European Research Program at the School of Advanced International Studies, Johns Hopkins University. *Foreign Policy*. 46:49–66. Spring '82. Reprinted with permission from *Foreign Policy*. Copyright © 1982 by the Carnegie Endowment for International Peace.

nents of the Reagan administration policy have yet to offer a credible explanation of what specific levers they would pull to force Poland's rulers and the Kremlin to retreat. For a variety of foreign policy and domestic reasons, the administration could not appear to stand idly by and conduct business as usual with the suppressors of Poland's freedom movement. Nevertheless, national leaders must carefully weigh desirable courses of action against the constraints of a given situation.

Thus the question is not whether the Reagan administration had to react to the imposition of martial law, but whether it chose the most effective and appropriate mix of steps in response. To answer this question observers must first assess what exactly happened in Poland and what role the Soviet Union has played there. Second, an accurate understanding of the Kremlin's behavior requires a close and objective look at Russian interests in, and commitments to, Poland. Third, Americans must evaluate in a cool and analytical fashion the nature and depth of U.S. interests in Poland. Finally, a realistic discussion of the foreign policy tools— military, economic, and diplomatic—available to U.S. policy makers in dealing with a political crisis deep within the Soviet orbit must precede any judgment of U.S. policy to date and any proposals for what Washington might do in the future.

Little doubt remains, as administration spokesmen have correctly observed, that the Soviet Union bears heavy responsibility for the suppression of Poland's peaceful revolution. Historians will probably argue for a long time over the degree to which Russia actually helped plan and impose martial law. The conspicuous but not unusual presence of Marshal Viktor Kulikov, the Warsaw Pact commander in chief, in the Polish capital just days before Jaruzelski's move against Solidarity appears to strengthen the argument that Moscow conceptualized and directed the coup. Furthermore, the fact that Jaruzelski had clearly prepared the crackdown well in advance would seem to indicate that, with Soviet connivance, he never seriously intended to achieve reconciliation with the independent labor union.

Yet there remain a number of ambiguities regarding both Jaruzelski's attitude toward Solidarity and Moscow's input into his decisions. The Soviet Union of course had an overriding influence on the environment within which the Warsaw government had to operate both before and after the crackdown. Poland's rulers could hardly have been unaware that the Kremlin did not posses unlimited patience. They knew that the Soviet Union would intervene if pushed too hard and that its list of victims would contain not only Solidarity's leaders but also those among Poland's Communist rulers who had allowed the situation to get out of control, including Jaruzelski himself.

Ample precedent existed for such actions. Most notorious, after the 1956 revolt, the Soviets ordered the execution of Hungarian leader Imre Nagy, whom they initially promised to support; and in 1968, after crushing what is called the Prague Spring in Czechoslovakia, the USSR orchestrated a major purge that removed Czech leader Alexander Dubcek and thousands of his supporters from power. Hence in 1981 Polish officialdom had good, selfish reasons to avoid losing Moscow's continued trust and to insure that the Soviet politburo did not act on its own.

By unleashing the Polish army and security services against Solidarity, Jaruzelski ran a considerably lesser risk. Even if he encountered stiffer opposition than expected and the crisis escalated into a civil war triggering Soviet intervention, the general and his colleagues would not lose completely. After all, the Kremlin would credit them with finally following its advice by cracking down on the independent labor union and other dissidents, including those inside the Communist party itself.

But the fact that the Soviets played a significant role in forcing Jaruzelski to crack down does not necessarily mean that the Polish elite did not have its own internal motives for stopping Solidarity's offensive. Nor does the army's masterful execution of martial law preclude the possibility that Jaruzelski and the Communist colonels and generals around him acted reluctantly and only after reaching the conclusion that all other options posed even greater dangers for themselves and their nation. In this sense, Mieczyslaw Rakowski, deputy prime minister, told the truth when following the crackdown he asserted that the Polish leadership had no good choices, only more terrible and less terrible ones.

At the time of the crackdown, Poland's economy lay in shambles. Jaruzelski and his associates could not ignore the shadow of a cold winter and the ever-growing threat of food riots. The regime needed to raise prices and to persuade or force farmers to sell their produce to the government. The country also needed a combination of economic reform, greater labor discipline, and considerable belt tightening. Any Polish government would have encountered difficulty accomplishing these tasks under the best conditions. For a discredited regime held in contempt by a majority of Poles and faced with a powerful domestic opposition—Solidarity—it became next to impossible.

A Gamble Pays Off

By the time Jaruzelski imposed martial law, both the union and the government had engaged in muscle flexing for several months. And while each side had made concessions and retreats, mutual disillusionment had grown steadily. In late September 1981, Solidarity's national convention became the scene of a radical revolt against union leader Lech Walesa, as opponents accused him of taking an excessively moderate line. In October Jaruzelski replaced Stanislaw Kania as secretary-general of the Communist Party, with an explicit mandate to assert his authority. By December positions had become so polarized that Walesa reportedly said, "Confrontation is inevitable and it will take place."

When the cadets at a fire-fighters' academy went on strike, which was crushed by force on December 2, the regime's alarm must have further increased. As one informed Polish official privately commented, "After all, in Iran it was the air cadets who put the last nail in the coffin of the old order." No regime struggling to survive can ignore the disintegration of its elite units. And the fire-fighting cadets—employees of the Ministry of Internal Affairs, which also supervises the police and internal troops—are elite troops. In the face of such defections, Jaruzelski may well have recalled V.I. Lenin's famous remark on the eve of the October Revolution: "Yesterday it was too early; tomorrow it will be too late."

Moreover, a majority of the Polish elite would have opposed surrender to the masses. In countries such as the Soviet Union and to a somewhat lesser degree Poland, the elites know they cannot outlive their Communist regimes. Party apparatchiks, central economic planners, and experts in Communist indoctrination would hardly fit comfortably into a new social setting. Hence, Poland's new elite felt threatened, even though some of its members may have favored reform and admired Solidarity. Jaruzelski accommodated their fears and their insecurities when he ordered martial law.

The growing disenchantment that many ordinary Poles began to feel with the course of events also figured in the regime's decision to crack down. During the 16 months between the founding of Solidarity and the imposition of martial law, social and economic conditions had steadily deteriorated in the country. Although few blamed the union, popular morale began to falter. Jaruzelski and his associates realized that the Polish people would not applaud martial law. But they hoped that taken by surprise and confronted with overwhelming force the Poles would not fight back. The gamble paid off.

The Soviets supported the gamble, but Jaruzelski claimed in his January 25, 1982, address to the Sejm that Soviet pressure did not lead to the imposition of martial law: "It was our own decision based on our own analysis and carried out with our own forces." Nevertheless, Soviet interference was well documented.

In March 1981, when Kania and then Prime Minister Jaruzelski visited Moscow, Soviet officials told them point blank that "the socialist community is indivisible and its defense is the concern not just of each individual state, but of the socialist coalition as a whole." On June 5, the Soviet leadership sent the Polish Central Committee a letter that in addition to advising Warsaw to "mobilize all healthy forces in society to resist the class enemy and to combat counterrevolution" reiterated the Kremlin's pledge not "to abandon a fraternal country in distress." In August Kania and Jaruzelski visited Soviet President Leonid Brezhnev. The Soviet leader promised additional economic aid but also reprimanded the Poles for being soft on "the threat of counterrevolution."

Then in mid-September a second, more threatening letter arrived from the Kremlin. According to Stefan Olszowski, one of the more hard-line Polish officials, the Soviet Union threatened to cut off its raw materials unless the situation improved. Reliable reports indicate that such Soviet pressure was a major factor in the October decision to replace Kania with Jaruzelski. These repeated threats and the periodic Warsaw Pact military maneuvers held in and around Poland provide clear evidence of deep Soviet involvement. Jaruzelski did not disappoint Moscow. Two months after his elevation as Polish Communist party leader, he introduced martial law.

Although Soviet connivance is beyond a reasonable doubt, to present Jaruzelski as a mere puppet blindly obeying the commands of his Kremlin masters would be an exaggeration. All available information about the general's background and views, including his earlier well publicized refusal to use the army against the striking workers, and about the military and civilian officials surrounding him tends to contradict such a conclusion. Soviet pressure was but one key factor Jaruzelski had to take into account. Soviet military intervention was probably inevitable had Jaruzelski refused to act. But at least in the short run, the Soviets were lucky. They found in Warsaw willing and capable accomplices, who partly for reasons of their own would serve as proxies.

Russia's View of Poland

Nobody could realistically expect the Kremlin to eschew any available tool short of force to restore law and order in Poland. Soviet interests in maintaining control over Poland are far too great for the Kremlin to allow Solidarity to undermine the very foundations of the Communist state. Five considerations colored the Soviet attitude toward the events in Poland.

First, Moscow has traditionally feared the threat a strong and independent Poland would pose for the preservation of the Russian empire. This fear involves a great deal of bitter history that has created unavoidable animosity between the Russians and the Poles. For centuries the two Slavic states fought for preeminence in Eastern Europe. At times the Poles controlled huge amounts of Russian and Ukrainian territory. At one point in the 17th century the Poles even managed to occupy Moscow and appointed in quick succession two of their Russian collaborators to the throne of Muscovy. In the 18th century Russia participated three times in the partitioning of Poland. In 1830 and in 1863 Russian troops put down courageous but hopeless Polish rebellions. Even their common struggle against Nazi Germany did not reduce the mutual hostility. Rather the Poles cannot forgive Moscow for its cynical decision to allow the Germans to crush the August 1944 Warsaw uprising.

In addition most Russians both under the czars and the Communists—even critics of those regimes—have harbored hostile feelings toward Poland. Reacting to Western outrage over the brutal suppression of Poland by the armies of Czar Nicholas, liberal-minded Russian poet Alexander Pushkin wrote in 1830 his famous poem "To the Slanderers of Russia," which supported the Russian action without reservation. Mikhail Bakunin, a revolutionary himself, said that "this is what the feelings of any Russian should be." Alexander Bestuzhev, persecuted and exiled for his participation in the 1825 Decembrist revolt, complained in a letter to his mother that he was deprived of a chance "to exchange gunshots" with the rebellious Poles. And during the 1863 Polish revolt most liberals with the exception of Alexander Herzen, a great Russian democrat and revolutionary, advocated liberty at home and the gallows for Polish freedom fighters abroad.

Centuries of oppression and bias do not legitimate the Soviet claims of a right to behave as the guardians of Poland's destiny. But many Russians and most members of the Russian elite do not consier Poland an independent state but rather some sort of an autonomous entity under Soviet supervision. As one Soviet put it, the Russian view of Poland resembles Israeli Prime Minister Menachem Begin's concept of Palestinian autonomy; publicly Soviet officials talk about a sovereign Poland, but in private conservations they occasionally refer to that country as "the Vistula provinces."

Second, Poland is crucial to the USSR's ability to maintain the post-World War II division of Europe. Vital communication links to East Germany run through Poland, making it indispensable for the maintenance of logistical support for Soviet forces in the German Democratic Republic. These forces, which include elite divisions, form the backbone of Moscow's military posture in Europe. The loss or destabilization of Poland would greatly increase the risk that North Atlantic Treaty Organization (NATO) forces could cut off these crack armies in the event of war. The alternative to maintaining firm control over Poland—to withdraw the forward divisions from East Germany—raises in Soviet eyes the frightening prospect of a unified Germany allied with the West. Thus for reasons of security Soviet leaders do not want their domination of Poland to end.

Third, the Kremlin fears that the Polish revolution will in the long run infect other East European countries as well. The economic difficulties that triggered the Polish rebellion exist throughout the Soviet bloc, even in Hungary, the most prosperous and successful Warsaw Pact country. Political alienation from Communist rule is also not limited to Poland. Probably no East European nation would willingly choose to retain its current Communist regime if given the choice. Hence, Moscow has reason to believe that unless it displays an iron fist in Poland, other East European countries might join the movement for a more open society and greater distance from the Soviet Union.

Fourth, the gradual collapse of the Communist party apparatus in Poland could not help but deeply disturb the Kremlin. What occurred in Poland essentially demonstrated the impotence and irrelevance of the Polish Communist party machinery. And the spectacle of the Polish Communist party—the vanguard of the working class—rejected and undermined by the workers themselves could only add to Soviet anxieties. Moreover, on the eve of the upcoming political succession in Moscow, the Soviet Communist party bureaucracy is least prepared to take a benign view of the destruction of the Communist party as a viable political force in a neighboring country.

Fifth, the Soviet Union in effect financed the Polish revolution, a fact that must have greatly increased Soviet frustration. The Polish renewal, so distasteful and threatening to Soviet elites, cost Russia billions of rubles in economic aid, loan rescheduling, and losses to the Soviet economy that resulted from Poland's inability to deliver contracted equipment and supplies in promised quantities and on schedule.

In the Soviet empire, contrary to all common economic sense, the conquerors subsidize the conquered. To justify the ever-growing burden of this unique imperialim, the Soviet elite expects at the minimum considerable political pay-offs; in Poland none existed. Instead, from the Russian perspective the vassals wanted to have their cake and eat it too. In theory the Brezhnev government could have warned Polish rulers to restore political and economic order quickly or suffer the aid cuts. This option, however, was never viable. For without Soviet economic aid, Polish leaders would have either faced political chaos and possibly civil war or accommodated Solidarity in the hope of receiving massive aid from the West. Moscow could not accept either scenario.

Debate over U.S. Leverage

The Brezhnev regime procrastinated for 16 months. This relative tolerance reflected the lack of any realistic Soviet options beyond military intervention as long as the Polish leadership itself refused to move against the independent union. In the end the Poles bailed the Soviets out by in essence invading themselves, albeit with direct Soviet complicity.

The legitimate U.S. desire not to allow Moscow to escape responsibility should not obscure the fact that the Soviets did not intervene militarily. Bearing in mind how much the Kremlin had at stake in Poland, Washington must realistically define U.S. interests there and formulate a pragmatic response. If the Soviets have committed a major encroachment on U.S. or Western interests or if the Western alliance has the means to influence either Soviet policies or at least their outcome, the West should seek to discipline Soviet power.

American interests in Poland are difficult to define. The debate in the United States regarding U.S. leverage and how best to use it has focused almost entirely on what responses to adopt and not sufficiently on the nature of U.S. interests. This narrow focus has resulted in greater confusion rather than increased clarity. Many critics of current U.S. policy, for example, compare Reagan's response to the crackdown in Poland with President Carter's response to the 1979 Soviet invasion of Afghanistan and imply that Carter reacted more firmly. Yet the two cases differ a great deal. In Afghanistan the Soviets mounted a massive invasion and executed President Hafizullah Amin, who had allegedly invited them in. In Poland, however, Soviet divisions stayed in their barracks while the Polish army and security units took over the country under the orders of a Polish leader whose legitimacy the West did not question.

Although Afghanistan has long been under heavy Soviet influence, it has never belonged to the Soviet bloc. The Soviet invasion represented a violation of the international status quo by force. Moreover, the Kremlin's action gave rise to widespread fears that Moscow intended to use Afghanistan as a transit station to the warm-water ports of the Persian Gulf—a region where the United States does have vital interests. Even those who dismissed—correctly, it appears—the notion that Moscow invaded Afghanistan because of its proximity to the Persian Gulf could not but recognize that Soviet aggression had yielded the Russians important military advantages in the region. Poland, however, lies within the Soviet East European empire. The restoration of Communist control over Poland preserves rather than alters the existing order there.

Of course, Westerners identify more closely with the suffering and struggle of Polish workers than with the tragedy and resistance of Afghan tribesmen. Poland, an integral part of Western civilization, has in recent months fought for the right to reestablish links with its cultural brethren. Nevertheless, the geopolitical implications of Soviet actions in Afghanistan and Poland are asymmetrical and require different Western reactions.

If the attempt to draw a parallel between Poland and Afghanistan is not appropriate, neither are comparisons with Hungary in 1956 and Czechoslovakia in 1968. Unlike in the latter two countries, the USSR did not intervene directly in Poland and did not remove from power local leaders who dissatisfied it. Only the future can tell whether the consequences of Jaruzelski's crackdown will resemble those of a Soviet military takeover. But to miss the distinction between Soviet complicity and outright Soviet aggression invites dangerous political errors. To label Jaruzelski a Soviet lackey and to tailor U.S. policy toward Poland accordingly without firm evidence to determine the hierarchy of his motives for cracking down—a fear of economic and social disorder, a desire to accommodate Moscow, the self-preservation of Poland's elite, and a sense that Warsaw had to pre-empt Soviet intervention—could turn an unsubstantiated, albeit plausible, charge into a self-fulfilling prophecy.

Thus, former Secretary of State Henry Kissinger's declaration that although the United States should be "forthcoming on Soviet strategic concerns" it must resist "the proposition that the Red Army is the guarantor of the irreversibility of history, the enforcer of the rule that what is Communist is eternal and what is non-Communist is fair game for undermining or worse" contains a serious flaw. For although the Red Army remained in the background in Poland and was a critical element in all assessments of the situation, it never acted as an actual enforcer.

Another explanation of why the United States should punish Brezhnev and Jaruzelski boils down to the claim that they have grossly violated the Helsinki accord. But this agreement is full of ambiguities that allow for a variety of incompatible interpretations. The Helsinki Final Act guarantees the basic human rights now brutally disregarded in Poland. But it also provides assurances that all states may conduct their domestic affairs without outside interference. Indeed the Polish leadership has complained that the United States, not the USSR, continually interferes in Poland.

Détente has steadily deteriorated since the Helsinki Final Act was signed in 1975. Many expected the accord to serve as a symbol of and as a contribution to the East-West rapprochement. Instead they have become a part of what Jeane Kirkpatrick, U.S. ambassador to the United Nations, calls the theater, where both sides charge each other with all possible and impossible violations. The Soviets certainly have not fulfilled their promises in the area of human rights, whereas the United States has failed to expand trade and scientific and cultural contacts. The United States can and should use the Helsinki document to attack Soviet repression in Poland. But to use the Final Act as a point of departure for defining American interests in Eastern Europe does not make sense. For it is ambivalent, self-contradictory, and based on wishful thinking.

Unwise Ultimatums

The neoconservative Committee for the Free World—free of communism but not necessarily from friendly right-wing dictators, of course—has offered the most coherent although not entirely persuasive definition of U.S. interests. The committee has blatantly recommended that America seek the disintegration of the Soviet empire. It does not explain, however, how America could achieve this commendable aim without provoking World War III. Implementation of the committee's casual suggestion to embargo practically all Western trade with the USSR and Poland would very likely lead to a resumption of the Cold War in its coldest period, a reintroduction of the Iron Curtain, and a tightening of Soviet control over Eastern Europe.

There is nothing God given about Soviet domination of Eastern Europe. And if the West can challenge that domination, it should. Neither the Yalta agreements nor any other international law preclude the West from sympathizing with and when possible actively supporting the aspirations of East European nations to throw off the Russian yoke or at least to win greater autonomy. The Western nations should also not allow Moscow to assume that they consider its sphere of influence sacrosanct, especially because the Russians do not hestitate to aid America's foes in the U.S. back yard. Few would dispute such points.

Much less agreement exists, however, regarding the wisdom of presenting Moscow with ultimatums: Grant more freedom to the East Europeans or the West will wage economic warfare against the Soviet Union and other Communist states. First, Russia has not shown any inclination to surrender to such blackmail. Second, Soviet interests in Eastern Europe, particularly in Poland, are so crucial that the Kremlin will endure almost any sanction rather than abandon control of its bloc.

The United States would, of course, welcome a decline of Moscow's control over Eastern Europe because such a development would slow the USSR's apparent global momentum. The Soviets themselves may eventually understand that their security and prosperity would gain from a less rigid and less heavy-handed relationship with Eastern Europe. After all, Russia enjoys friendly and economically profitable relations with its democratic neighbor Finland. Soviet leaders are not reflexive interventionists. They reconciled themselves to economic reforms in Hungary. They never seriously threatened Romania, despite the fact that it criticized the Soviet invasion of Czechoslovakia, assisted Sino-American rapprochement, and has pursued an independent Middle East policy.

In Poland, Moscow for decades accepted an independent Catholic church and greater domestic political pluralism than anywhere else in the Soviet orbit. Solidarity went too far and too fast for the Kremlin and for a considerable segment of the Polish elite as well. But the chapter opened by the independent union has not necessarily ended. The United States would best serve its own interests by encouraging Moscow and Warsaw to move toward reconciliation with the Polish people. And in the event that reconciliation does not work, the United States should not fire all its policy bolts at once; otherwise Moscow and Warsaw will conclude that further repression will not have any new and serious repercussions.

Successfully Avoiding Extremes

These U.S. interests are important but not vital. For vital interests are those a nation will defend by all means, including if necessary by military force. In evaluating U.S. alternatives in dealing with the Polish situation, Washington must recognize that it has no military options and that the Russians know this. Given the lack of military options, U.S. policy should have clearly defined objectives. It should also be reasonably cost effective in economic and political terms. As one observer put it: Unless they are cost effective, "embargo policies resemble a tiger without teeth or claws, a tiger unable to do more than growl a little. This will impress only the simple-minded and will do so only for a short time."

The Reagan administration had to furmulate its policies toward the Polish crisis within fairly narrow margins. Both doing nothing and doing too little would have invited harsh domestic criticism. The experience of the 1970s demonstrated that Washington cannot maintain a multidimensional and calibrated policy toward the USSR if the U.S. public perceives that policy as appeasing aggressors or surrendering principles. Too weak a response would also send a wrong signal to the Poles and other East Europeans instead of reminding them that America supports their aspirations for dignity and self-determination. But the absence of effective military tools and the predictable reluctance of the allies to join in harsh measures against the USSR limit the range of responses available to U.S. policy makers.

The Reagan administration deserves credit in its initial policy response for successfully avoiding the extremes. Secretary of State Alexander Haig, Jr. exhibited common sense and courage when he refused to submit to demands for a far more massive response than the circumstances permitted. Creating an artificial crisis in the alliance in response to the Polish tragedy would benefit only the Soviet Union. To insist recklessly that the West Europeans participate in sanctions that they consider neither wise nor fair would only transform a crisis within the Warsaw Pact into an unnecessary and dangerous crisis within NATO.

Unfortunately, under heavy pressure from parochial and messianic unilateralists, the administration was hardly in a position to deliberate calmly as it tried to choose the best possible mix of steps in its response to the Polish crackdown. No measures the United States could realistically have adopted would have led to a return to the pre-martial-law situation in Poland. Ideally, before formulating its policies, Washington should have decided whether it was prepared to settle for anything less than a return to the status quo before the crackdown and if so what outcome it would view as acceptable. Administration strategists did not adequately address these questions before they proceeded with their package of limited economic sanctions against the USSR and Poland. The cancellation of Aeroflot flights and restrictions on the access of Soviet ships in U.S. ports do not mean much. More significant, however, the United States once again adopted economic sanctions before it had sufficiently exploited other diplomatic means.

Essentially three types of sanctions exist: those that retard, those that influence, and those that punish. The United States, for example, has every reason to want to retard Soviet military capabilities. Thus, regardless of the course of events in Poland, tightening controls over the transfer of sensitive Western technology to the USSR makes sense.

Sanctions designed to influence a foreign nation are most effective when implicit rather than explicit and positive rather than negative. Such sanctions usually require considerable leverage as well as a realistic appraisal of how the target country will perceive the costs and benefits of giving in to or resisting the pressure. As a rule, sanctions will influence behavior only on issues of less than vital interest to the country on which they are imposed. The marginal sanctions adopted by Reagan hardly suffice to influence Polish and Soviet policy concerning an interest as vital as the survival of communism in Poland.

Punitive sanctions serve primarily to send strong signals of displeasure and warning and often require that the country imposing them incur costs itself to demonstrate the depth of its resolve. Caius Mucius Scaevola, for example, held his hand in a flame to impress upon the Etruscans Rome's determination to resist invasion. The Etruscans were impressed and withdrew. But that occurred outside Rome, a city with high walls and well-trained legions. Watergate participant G. Gordon Liddy considered himself Scaevola's disciple, but he lacked the Etruscans, the walls, and the legions. When he burned his hand, he was merely considered ridiculous and rightly so.

Thus, punitive sanctions send effective messages only when they involve a credible threat of escalation to a level sufficient to stop the offender. In the case of Poland, America's limited sanctions do not pass the test. Instead, Washington's casual use of marginal sanctions, which the West Europeans did not support and never were expected to support, succeeded only in communicating America's sense of frustration and impotence.

Rely on Diplomacy

The United States could adopt two economic measures that would severely hurt the Soviet Union and the Jaruzelski regime. Washington could allow Poland to default on its loans. Although this policy would succeed in creating enormous problems for the martial law government, it would also bring about a number of highly unwelcome consequences. Faced as a result with an economic catastrophe, Jaruzelski would have no choice but to rely on draconian steps to maintain domestic order. Any hope of eventual accommodation and compromise internally would be lost. In addition, Warsaw would find itself totally at Moscow's mercy, forced to offer absolute political obedience in exchange for desperately needed Soviet economic assistance. Ordinary people, includng Solidarity members, would obviously suffer greatly from both starvation and oppression. A Polish default would inevitably affect other East European countries as well. Western bankers would view them all as bad credits risks, and they would have to become more heavily dependent on the USSR. Finally, a Polish default would hurt the West Europeans far more than the American government and banks. It might as a result give new impetus to anti-Americanism and neutralism in Western Europe. A default might even do permanent damage to the world's credit structure.

Second, Washington could impose a grain embargo. The Reagan administration erred in April 1981 when, despite intense Soviet pressure on Poland but after repeated false alarms of invasion, it lifted the grain embargo Carter had imposed on the Soviet Union to protest the invasion of Afghanistan. To reinstitute it now simply because this very same pressure against Poland combined with other factors finally succeeded would only illustrate the inconsistencies of U.S. foreign policy. And if a grain embargo did not persuade the Soviets to leave Afghanistan, it will certainly not change their behavior regarding Poland. And angry U.S. farmers would eventually demand the end of the embargo, tempting the administration to retreat once again in the face of Soviet resolve.

Of course, any future economic aid to Poland should be contingent upon the significant relaxation of police controls and the resumption of meaningful discussions with the opposition—Solidarity and the Catholic church. Only if considerable progress toward resolution of the crisis occurs can the United States help pull Poland through the difficult economic period ahead. The United States cannot break the Soviet empire, but it can and should refrain from subsidizing Moscow's efforts to maintain it through force and repression.

In addition, the United States should rely more heavily on diplomacy. A postponement of the meeting between Haig and Soviet Foreign Minister Andrei Gromyko, for example, would definitely have attracted Moscow's attention. The argument that especially in times of crisis the White House and the Kremlin must engage in dialogue is unpersuasive. Poland is not a crisis in the U.S-Soviet relationship that requires this kind of dialogue. For unlike the October 1973 Middle East war, the current events do not threaten a direct military confrontation between the superpowers.

A U.S. withdrawal from the Helsinki process would send an even more powerful message. Two arguments are usually mentioned in favor of preserving the process: first, that it provides an effective forum for exposing Soviet human rights violations and, second, that the West Europeans still believe that it can contribute to détente. Concerning the first point, any performance repeated often enough eventually loses its impact on the audience. The endless criticisms of Soviet repression have become a matter of routine and have ceased even to be good theater. Some West Europeans, most notably the West Germans, would complain if the United States abandoned the negotiations. Yet they would probably prefer this to endless American pressures to join U.S. sanctions. After all, the postwar border settlement and the status of Berlin are already guaranteed by other, more binding and less controversial agreements than the Helsinki Final Act. Most important, the West Europeans would not remain in the process without the United States.

The United States could do little to prevent a Polish tragedy. And America has only limited leverage to change current Polish and Soviet policies. Yet if Washington uses this limited leverage skillfully, it can cement the unity of the NATO alliance and force Brezhnev and Jaruzelski to exhibit greater flexibility. Both Moscow and Warsaw seem at this point to be reacting to events rather than following a well-thought-out plan. Even the future structure of the Polish leadership remains unclear. It will probably resemble something in between a traditional Communist party dictatorship and a Communist nationalist military junta. But here matters a degree do count, and the West can affect them with strong U.S. leadership. If America abuses its leverage, the double disaster of

a U.S. policy failure and increased alliance tension could be added
to the Polish tragedy.

III. MARTIAL LAW AND AFTER

EDITOR'S INTRODUCTION

The imposition of martial law in Poland, which occurred without warning on the night of December 13, 1981, put an end to the immediate dilemma facing the leaders of the Soviet Union, but did nothing to resolve the problems that had led to the rebellion. The Poles returned reluctantly to work, Walesa and his colleagues were jailed, and the Solidarity movement was suppressed, but the Polish economy remains a shambles and shortages of food and raw materials are acute. The threat of a Soviet invasion has receded, or even vanished, but there is no evidence that the suppression of the Poles by their own army, rather than by a foreign power, has done anything to heal the division between the government and the people. There can be little doubt that the Polish crisis marked an important stage in the evolution of Communism, but its ultimate consequences have yet to appear.

The third section of this compilation describes and analyzes the present social, political, and economic state of Poland. The first article, from *U.S. News and World Report,* describes the military crackdown and swift suppression of dissent. Secondly, a report from the *Wall Street Journal* assesses the Polish government's chances of building a recovery on Poland's principal resource, coal. The third article, from *Commonweal,* describes the circumstances of the Pope's second visit to Poland in 1983, and concludes that the church, whose influence on Polish affairs remains unchallenged by Communism, will continue to advise moderation in the hope of achieving gradual change. Reports from the *New York Times* and *Wall Street Journal* evoke the bitterness and humorous resignation of the Polish intelligentsia, and the depressed and disorganized condition of the Polish Communist Party. John Darnton, who won a Pulitzer Prize for his reporting on Poland, relates the events of the past three years in a personal diary from the *New York Times Magazine* and, in the final article, a *Los Angeles*

Times reporter recounts the latest in a long series of conflicts between the Polish people and their government.

AS LAST HOPES FOR FREEDOM DWINDLE IN POLAND[1]

A cloud of dark despair engulfs this troubled land as the realization sinks in that there can be no quick easing of tough Communist rule under Poland's no-nonsense military men.

With the arrival of spring, the defiant slogan once hurled at Gen. Wojciech Jaruzelski's martial-law regime—"The winter is yours, the spring will be ours"—now seems to be mere bravado.

Resistance to the ruling Communist generals has faded to little more than a war of leaflets. Morale of the people is sinking to rock bottom as repression and economic deprivation take their toll. Freedom that once appeared so close now is an unobtainable goal.

Pessimism is strong even among the military officers and hardline Communist Party officials who took over last December 13 after crushing Solidarity, the independent labor movement that had led the 16-month-long drive for democratic reform here.

One leading Communist concedes that the crackdown against Solidarity has alienated workers needed to get industrial production back on track. Deputy Prime Minister Mieczyslaw Rakowski describes the economy as being in a state of collapse. A well-informed diplomat predicts that if martial law were lifted tomorrow, "Poland could easily break apart, because there is no government or Communist Party structure left."

Prospects of reconciling the nation's feuding factions are virtually nonexistent. More than 3,000 Solidarity leaders remain under arrest, including Lech Walesa, the symbol of Poland's unprecedented experiment with reform. Church-state relations in this intensely Roman Catholic country also are becoming more bitter as the regime spurns calls for easing military rule.

[1]Reprint of an article by Robin Knight, correspondent. *U.S. News & World Report.* 92:33–4. Mr. 29, '82. Copyright © U.S. News & World Report, Inc.

Outside pressures from the West and East are mounting.
Western Europe and the U.S are tightening economic sanctions
aimed at forcing Polish rulers into lifting martial law. The Soviet
Union, in turn, makes clear that it expects Jaruzelski to take
whatever harsh measures are needed to preserve Poland's allegiance to Moscow.

Jaruzelski's military rule is evident everywhere, especially in
the capital, where 40,000 Polish troops are deployed to keep its
1.5 million people in line. Warsaw resembles a city at war.

Half-frozen soldiers patrol the shabby streets. Tanks and armored vehicles sit ready to move at an instant. A nighttime curfew
remains in force. Documents are checked constantly and carefully.
Military commissars with powers of arbitrary arrest run the factories. Even television newscasts are read by Army officers.

The heavy hand of the Communist state is apparent in many
other ways.

A purge of "unreliable" Communist officials—recalling those
of the Stalinist era—is under way. Crucifixes have been ripped
from the walls of schoolrooms. The study of Marxism-Leninism
once again is part of the mandatory curriculum. A prerecorded
message reminds telephone users that calls are monitored. Official
permission is needed to photocopy any papers.

Particularly apparent to an outsider is the marked drop-off in
contacts between Poles and visiting Westerners. Comments one
observer: "Outright fear has taken a firm hold here in Poland."

There has been a slight relaxation of controls since the darkest
days of winter. Travel around Poland is allowed. The state-run
radio has resumed broadcasts of Sunday Mass. But as Jaruzelski's
Military Council of National Salvation reminds everyone Poland
remains in a "state of war."

Reinforcing the regime's defensive stance are economic sanctions imposed by Western nations. Although regarded as mild in
the West, they are blamed here for contributing to a host of economic difficulties, from lack of poultry to an absence of lightbulbs.

And while some Poles see the Western embargoes as a demon-
stration of support and sympathy, others worry that the sanctions
are driving Poland more firmly into the hands of Russia. Says a
university professor: "Please tell the world that we are desperate
to keep our links with the West alive."

Whatever the effect of the Western embargoes, there is no doubt that this nation is fast becoming an economic basket case. The bleak scene:

• Poland is as close to bankruptcy as it is possible to get without going over the brink. Foreign debts exceed 28 billion dollars. Polish officials announced on March 16 [1982] that they had completed payment of interest on the country's 1981 debt, but Warsaw will need 10 billion dollars in hard currency to meet 1982 obligations. No one knows where the money will come from.

• Living standards fell by 25 percent in 1981 and will decline by as much again this year [1982]. Streets are eerily empty and car parks full because gasoline is rationed along with food.

• Industrial output, down 23 percent last year [1981], dropped 12 percent more in January and February. Short of raw materials and spare parts, factories are working at 60 percent of capacity. The huge foreign debt makes it all but impossible to seek help from the West.

• Prices are up 200 to 300 percent, raised by the government in a campaign to cut back subsidies and encourage production. Some foods, such as ham, butter and sugar, now cost four times more than they did in January.

• The zloty, the national currency, is practically worthless. Since the start of 1982, it has been devalued 135 percent against the dollar. One result: Poles are unloading their money and buying whatever goods they can find. In turn, that is reducing the supplies of such scarce goods as meat.

Heightening the sense of disillusionment is the shattering blow dealt to the independent-labor-union movement.

Today, scarcely a Solidarity leader of importance is free. [Most have since been released. Ed.] The organization's Warsaw headquarters is shuttered, its nationwide structure destroyed. If Solidarity survives at all—and its chances are slim—it will be through small cells that operate clandestinely.

Still, the regime's efforts to discredit Solidarity in the eyes of the Polish worker seem to be getting nowhere. Recent official surveys asking workers what kind of union they favored overwhelmingly produced a stock three-word reply: "Solidarity and Walesa."

Nor is there any sign that attempts to crush the spirits of the interned Solidarity leaders are succeeding. When the government recently offered to grant internees a one-way passport out of Poland, only 50 out of 3,953 accepted the deal. By every account, opposition to the regime among the internees is hardening. "Internment is an open wound," says Wladyslaw Fiszdon, vice president of Warsaw University. "If it changes opinions, it is certainly not in the government's direction."

The regime's response to the rising hostility is twofold. It is cutting off serious dialogue with Solidarity leaders and it is putting out word that the movemnet, technically only under suspension, actually is finished.

Creating still more tensions in Poland are worsening church-government relations, crucial to any lasting settlement of the crisis. Long a force for moderation between the deeply religious Poles and their Communist bosses, the church under Archbishop Josef Glemp has pursued a critical but restrained line since the imposition of martial law. But in mid-March the primate demanded, for the first time, the release of Solidarity leader Walesa. Now pressure is mounting on Glemp to take an even tougher stance.

For Jaruzelski, the confrontation with the church and Solidarity and the sagging economy are not the only problems demanding attention. An equal worry is disarray within the Polish Communist Party, known officially as the Polish United Workers Party.

It was liberal-minded party members linked with Solidarity who, starting in 1981, first overhauled the party, introducing democratic reforms unprecedented in the Communist world. Then the military took over, triggering yet another shake-up. In just two years, the party's entire leadership, except for Jaruzelski, has been purged or disgraced. The party's youth movement has disintegrated. One in every 5 rank-and-file members has walked out. Since December, some 2,750 top officials have been swept from power. Former leader Edward Gierek faces a political show trial later this year.

The party today, says Deputy Prime Minister Rakowski, is "bankrupt intellectually and politically, unable to organize society." Adds a senior Western diplomat: "The party's whole structure has been crippled. At the moment, it certainly is in no shape to take over from the military."

Faced with deadlock and intransigence at every turn, Jaruzelski seems more and more intent on imposing his own authoritarian solutions on Poland.

Central to this tough-minded strategy, diplomatic observers say, is the deal that Jaruzelski struck with the Kremlin in early March. In return for emergency aid worth 1.5 billion dollars, Poland is to end its flirtation with the West and return to Moscow's fold.

Russians Move In

Already some elements of the shift are under way. Poland will increase sharply this year its reliance on Soviet raw materials, parts and markets. Russian advisers are to move into government ministries, as they did in Afghanistan after the Soviets' 1979 invasion there. Polish links with the West are being downgraded.

Politically, top priority is being given to the rebuilding of an orthodox Communist Party to be run by a small elite backed up by a potent police apparatus. Liberal reforms introduced last year have been shelved. Officials who cooperated with Solidarity are losing their jobs to hard-liners.

All that is a long way from uniting the country, however. In the words of one high-ranking Western diplomat: "The generals underestimated Poland's problems and overestimated their capacity to solve them."

The array of challenges confronting the regime is awesome— parlous economic conditions, strong popular support for Solidarity, unwillingness of the union's leaders to buy the government line, growing opposition of the church and weakness of the Communist Party.

With no easy solutions in sight, an end to martial law is not in the cards. Jaruzelski's grip on the country is so tight that organized resistance seems out of the question. But with deepening discontent, it is equally clear that Poland will remain one of Moscow's major headaches and a lasting source of friction with the U.S. and the West.

SILESIAN GOLD: POLAND COUNTS ON COAL TO
CURE ECONOMIC ILLS, BUT OBSTACLES REMAIN[2]

Katowice, Poland—The sky here is almost always grimy gray,
as if the coal dust from the mines below has become lodged in the
air above.

Katowice and much of the flat, characterless 100-square mile
area around it rest upon a honeycomb of coal mines—Poland's
economic heartland. Coal is the country's dearest asset and biggest
earner of foreign currency. However, it also causes Polish authorities a lot of problems, of which the stubborn smog may be the most
tractable.

Katowice is sinking. Buildings have cracked; roads have
sagged and at least one river has been unintentionally redirected,
as the city gradually has settled above its mines. The old airport
is closed to commercial planes because sinkage has made its landing strip something of a roller coaster.

"Nowhere in the world can you find so much coal under a
built-up area," remarks Kazimierz Sluzewski, the deputy director
of the Katowice colliery, one of 66 working mines in the Silesia
region. He tramps through the warm, moist, dusty tunnels of his
mine, then stops and sighs: "This is where the Holy Mother put
the coal."

Poland has seldom been so determined to get coal out of the
ground. The country desperately needs the hard currency coal exports provide to buy Western spare parts and commodities and to
assuage Western bankers. It needs the coal at home to fuel 80%
of Poland's industry and to generate 95% of its electricity. However, many observers feel that Polish authorities have been so eager
to increase extraction that they have overlooked the attendant human and financial costs.

Deaths in coal-mining accidents last year increased at a faster
rate than coal output did. Investigators from Poland's central min-

[2]Reprint of an article by Frederick Kempe, staff reporter. *Wall Street Journal.* 202:1+. Ag. 8, '83. Reprinted by permission of the *Wall Street Journal.* Copyright © Dow Jones & Company, Inc. 1983. All rights
reserved.

ing office recently conceded that basic safety precautions were at times ignored in 1982.

On the financial side, Poland's production costs are unusually high. However, its domestic prices are set artificially low and its international suppliers undercut world prices so as to win markets. The net result is that the industry operates in the red.

"Poland would like the world to see its coal industry as the one true economic success story of martial law," remarks a Western diplomat in Warsaw who studies the Polish economy. "However, the truth isn't that rosy. The industry has serious problems that must be corrected."

Correcting them is essential; coal is crucial to Poland's economic hopes. Successful mining operations would also provide Poland its greatest chance of luring back badly needed Western credits and eventually of repaying rescheduled loans.

Disciplined Mines

Poland's martial-law government understandably designated coal as its top priority after it put down the Solidarity trade union 20 months ago. It since has boasted of increased output from strictly disciplined mines, which had been militarized earlier.

Poland extracted 95.2 million tons of coal in the first half of this year, half a million tons more than in the like period of 1982, and 2.4 million tons more than it had intended. Polish officials are confident that this year they will far exceed last year's output of 189.3 million tons, which itself was almost a 20% increase from 1981.

More than half of Poland's exported coal would go to Western countries for hard currency. Most of the rest would go to the Soviet Union, largely in exchange for oil. Polish suppliers have been recapturing foreign markets lost to South African, Australian and U.S. suppliers, among others, when 1981 strikes cut production and forced Poland to renege on contracts. The country has exported as much coal—16.6 million tons—in the first six months of this year as it did during all of 1981.

Gen. Wojciech Jaruzelski's martial-law government hence beams that it has restored Poland to a secure position as the world's fourth-largest exporter of coal (after the U.S.). Officials also are confident about the future. The 120 billion tons of coal in Poland's reserves could keep production at current levels for the next 600 years.

A Losing Business

But first Poland must figure out how to make coal profitable. "Coal mining, the national industry which could get Poland's economic recovery under way, turns out to be operated at a loss," said an article recently in Polityka, a respected Polish weekly newspaper.

"The cost of mining the coal exceeds by about 10% the price the industry gets for it, and that cost is growing," the article says. "As a result, the industry receives even bigger state subsidies."

Coal industry sources say that between 1971 and 1980, the average price for Polish coal increased by as little as 30% while extraction costs grew 130%. The Polityka article avers that costs exceeded revenues by nearly 73% in 1980.

There are several reasons for the high costs. First, almost all of Polish coal mining is underground rather than open-pit mining. Second, repairing damage caused by subsidence and tunneling is said to cost $110 million to $170 million annually.

Moreover, Poland uses what is known as "sand backstowing" to refill exploited coal seams. It invented the costly method and is the only country that makes much use of it. The method entails refilling spent mines by pumping in water and sand. The water is then pumped out, and the sand remains. According to the mining ministry sinkage is thereby restricted to just five feet per 50 feet mined, less than a third of the subsidence old procedures allowed. Mining experts nonetheless estimate that Katowice will sink more than 10 feet over the next 40 years.

Poles use 30 million cubic meters of sand each year and, to transport it, have built a rail system that is one-fourth the size of the national railway.

"We and most other countries could never afford to use such a system," comments John Mills, the deputy chairman of the British National Coal Board. "The difference is that those in Poland responsible for production aren't also responsible for sales, so they don't have to worry about operating profitably."

What irks Mr. Mills and others is that despite these high costs, the Poles for years have undercut world prices in order to win markets. "It's regarded as a bit unfair," says Mr. Mills. "Naturally, one has been concerned."

Preferential Treatment

Another reason for high mining costs is that Polish miners are by far the best-rewarded industrial workers in Poland. The average salary at the Katowice colliery is nearly three times the average Polish salary. The government also provides miners a meat ration of 15.5 pounds per month, nearly three times what other workers get.

Miners are also given access to special stores, which stock goods unavailable to other Poles, such as radios, color televisions, furniture, clothing and shoes.

The extra privileges reflect the government's recognition of miners' difficult and dangerous work in the nation's most-vital industry. There are political reasons, too. The martial-law government—apparently with some success—is trying to buy the allegiance of miners, who as members of Solidarity had fiercely resisted martial law. At least seven miners were shot at Katowice's Wujek mine in the first days of martial law.

"I wouldn't say we are so privileged," says Kazimierz Karczewski, who at 38 has worked underground for 20 years. He hardly looks privileged in the layer of black dust that covers his helmet, his face, his uniform and even his teeth as he toils in the semi-darkness beside the whirring blades gouging the coal face. "I think our leaders have been educated as to how difficult our task is," he says.

And dangerous. A confidential document of the mining ministry's obtained through unofficial channels shows that there were 144 deaths in coal-mining accidents last year, or about 0.78 death for each one million tons extracted. That is more than twice the rate of such fatalities in Britain and compares poorly with 89 deaths the year before in Poland, when Solidarity's safety-first campaign reduced mining fatalities to their lowest point in more than a decade.

The mining industry says fatalities this year are far fewer, but authorities won't provide statistics. "The situation is considerably better," says Mr. Sluzewski of the Katowice colliery. His mine last December had its first fatal accident in three years. "After the accidents of last year, more severe regulations came out, and there now are more frequent safety controls," he says.

Each major accident results in several days of nervousness in the mines and an increase in sick leave. Miners stop more often to pray outside the colliery before the statue of St. Barbara, the patron of coal miners. She has been a fixture outside mines since the advent of Solidarity, when the union demanded and got her altar placed outside all mines.

However, she and even many safety measures can't change Polish geography. Edward Mecha, the president of Katowice, whose grandfather died in a coal-mining accident, says that safety procedures are good but that many Polish mines are inherently dangerous because they are so deep and subject to earth tremors.

Lax Safety Procedures

International experts, however, also charge that the Poles in their haste don't put up proper supports or "safety pillars" of earth to buttress ceilings and prevent rocks from falling on working miners.

"They don't have the same engineering and safety standards we have," says Mr. Mills of the British coal board.

Mr. Sluzewski of the Katowice mine says authorities have scrimped on safety. For example, he says that rubber on conveyer belts transporting coal out of the mine isn't properly fire resistant. Moreover, insulation for high-voltage wiring isn't adequate. A spark could thus ignite gases and cause an explosion.

Miners themselves only reluctantly speak of safety matters with outsiders. However, a Katowice priest says many come to him privately to express fears and to ask for help. Miners are among the most religious of Poles and begin each work day by exchanging the greeting "Sczcesc Boze," roughly translated as "God's luck be with you."

On his most recent trip to Poland, Pope John Paul II chose Katowice as the site for his workers Mass, which drew nearly 1.5 million people.

He spoke of the coal-mining accidents and of miners killed in resisting martial law: "Let us remember all the deceased workers, those who were the victims of mortal accidents in the mines or in other places—those who lost their lives in recent tragic events. All of them."

He bade farewell to the cheering crowd by shouting, "Sczcesc Boze." The crowd repeated the phrase again and again.

THE POPE AND POLAND: AND NOW WHAT?
RESISTANCE, NOT REBELLION[3]

In May [1983], Cardinal Jozef Glemp, Poland's Primate, told journalists in Rome that both the church and the government were ready to receive the pope "if others allow it." On one level, the second pilgrimage was "allowed." But with the crowds having dispersed and the pope back in Rome, everyone in and out of Poland is asking "What now?"

The pope's visit was an unusual event. It is not unusual for John Paul to travel to distant countries. Nor is it unusual for him to address enormous numbers of people. What was unusual about the June 16–23 [1983] journey was (1) that his listeners—who in several cities numbered in the millions—not only heard, but understood the pope, and not merely his text, but everything that was implied between the lines and everything that was omitted; (2) that the visit was so unabashedly political (the more the Polish authorities and the Vatican denied its political character, the more apparent its social and political dimensions became); and (3) that the pope came to Poland at an unusual moment in that country's history, a period of "post-martial law." Officially introduced on

[3]Reprint of an article by Thomas E. Bird, Director of the Council for the Study of Ethics and Public Policy at Queens College, New York. *Commonweal.* 110:390-2. Jl. 15, '83. Reprinted by permission.

December 13, 1981, martial law has in fact remained in force until today, although under another name.

Martial law was introduced in order to suppress the most massive people's movement in the history of Europe—Solidarity, the
fledging free-labor movement. What a paradox that in 1980 in
Catholic Poland the dream of Marxists world-wide was realized:
industrial workers became the leading force in the transformation
of a society. There was only one small problem with the *praxis*
from a socialist viewpoint: the workers achieved this victory not
against a bourgeois, but against a socialist government! This
workers' movement—which, with remarkable speed, became a
national movement—enjoyed the cooperation and support of the
Catholic intellectuals and many segments of the Catholic establishment.

When the leaders of Solidarity, with Lech Walesa at their
head, swore their allegiance to the church (in the words of a traditional Polish vow) "by word and sword," the church uncondition-
ally embraced the movement and, somewhat belatedly, joined the
national trend. When Solidarity was suppressed, and the impact
of martial law was felt in every facet of Polish life, the position
of the church became uncomfortable. Many of the liberties which
the church had enjoyed were threatened. The hierarchy, headed
by Cardinal Glemp, understood better than the man-in-the-street
that martial law had been introduced at the inspiration of Moscow
and with the close cooperation of the Kremlin, which was firmly
committed to the suppression of any visible or violent resistance
against the new Polish regime. (This understanding about the
danger of the involvement of "others" had also been the basis of
cooperation between the Gomulka and the Gierek regimes and the
Catholic church.) What the subjective intentions were of the Party
and government leaders who granted to the Polish church concessions greater than those in any other socialist country is debatable.
But clearly both parties were interested in social discipline, civic
responsibility, and the economic development of the nation; and
both wanted to avoid a debacle of the Hungarian and Czech type
which would not, in Poland, have been as peaceful as in those
neighboring lands and could have evolved into a catastrophe for
the nation.

After the institution of General Jaruzelski's military dictatorship, the church had to decide whether it was time to change its attitude towards the state authorities or to continue some cooperation of the sort that had existed until then. A Hobson's choice. The church had to choose between continuing a policy of appeasement, thereby losing the confidence of Poland's patriots, or adding its powerful voice of criticism to the opposition and, eventually, assuming a large share of the moral responsibility for unrest, which could have led to an open uprising against the regime, which could have led to. . . .

The balancing-and-postponement techniques practiced by the primate evoked strong and widespread criticism within Poland. Many observers feared that the centuries-old identification of Catholicism and Polishness could break apart. The memory and spirit of the anti-Russian uprisings in Poland in 1830 and 1963 were abroad in the land even as the Vatican condemned rebellion against legitimate political authority. Meanwhile, the lower-ranking clergy—who were from the people—stood with the people. The politicization of parishes and of church services became a volatile fact of life in Poland, a fact duly noted by both government and hierarchy.

As John Paul prepared for this trip, he had to reflect on the changes which had taken place in his homeland since his first visit in 1979. During that pilgrimage his pastoral messages recommended the preservation of law and order and praised hard work and frugality. For his part, First Secretary Gierek emphasized that relations between the church and the state had entered a phase of cooperation, which he defined as everything which serves the development of Poland and helps to strengthen its security and its position in the international arena, furthers progress in social life, and undergirds the family. The government perceived the pope's remarks as a great boost for its economic plans and the people accepted these admonitions, knowing that they were the price of the relative religious freedom which they—in distinction from the citizens of other socialist countries—enjoyed.

Manifestly, the same slogan—*ora et labora*—would in 1983 have smacked of collaboration. John Paul had to avoid even the possibility of such an inference being made. On the other hand, if he limited himself to a summons to prayer, this would have implied an abdication of the earthly kingdom and a retreat to the spiritual sphere. No pope could have afforded to give back such a message—certainly not a Polish pope in his native land.

He could have postponed his trip, but apparently no one wanted that. The government was anxious for some kind of legitimization. (The hierarchy needed legitimization and encouragement as well.) Thus, the pope found himself called upon to give his blessing to two contradictory interests. He seems to have decided that his only option was a radical one: to take the offensive and speak bluntly.

Defying the government, the pope reminded them that the Poles have a right to know the truth, that they have the right to a decent life, that they should have the right to form their own independent trade unions. Here he referred to his own encyclical, *Laborem exercens,* which is better known and more appreciated in Poland than in other western countries. And in the style of Jean Jacques Rousseau, he reminded the powers-that-be that the people have an inalienable right to freedom.

But he didn't give a full and unqualified blessing to the hierarchy's stance up until now either. Admonishing them to be persistent in their work for freedom, he was obviously appealing to all those Poles who feel oppressed and dispirited to lift up their hearts. Indeed, *sursum corda* was the main refrain of John Paul's 1983 pilgrimage.

What, in the practical order, can the upshot be of such encouragement conveyed to millions who are in contention with the political establishment? The pope made clear in so many words that the government is violating divine laws and human rights. His listeners had to ask themselves whether that is sufficient reason for open resistance against oppression and, if so, what form this resistance might take. He left open the question of what the people should do in order to compel the government to fulfill its obligations and the written social contract of September 1980—the agreements between the Polish government and the striking workers which have birth to autonomous trade unions. This was in fact the only concrete advice he gave: Return to Solidarity. Return to the agreements which have been violated by the military government.

But defiance of these agreements is the *raison d'être* of the present military government. Can the pope reasonably expect that the government will commit some act of political self-annihilation—assuming that the Soviet Union, "the others," would permit such an act? Not in the wake of Andrei Gromyko's carefully-timed reminder that Poland is an integral part of the socialist commonwealth. According to the Brezhnev Doctrine, that means that the five thousand tanks in East Germany and the twenty-eight divisions just east of the Polish frontier have a clear and present role in the life of today's Poland.

The Poles face a problem dealt with centuries ago by the Fathers of the church and elaborated in greater detail by St. Thomas Aquinas. What should people do when the government is obviously violating natural law? First, the people have to consider whether rebellion—an evil in itself—will be a greater good than the toleration of the existing evil. Second, if the answer is positive, they must consider whether there is any real chance of success, and if so, whether this is the appropriate moment to defy the government.

Application of the Angelic Doctor's teaching to present circumstances would indicate that since there is no prospect of success—inasmuch as the military government is supported by the entire might of the Soviet armed forces—one should refrain for the time being from open defiance, looking for ways of assuring national survival until the time is more apposite for action.

The role of the church—and her shepherds—should be to serve as a kind of guide helping the nation to find the best way to overcome the current political, economic, and intellectual crisis. Polish Catholicism is well equipped for this task. Thousands of educated Catholics perform various important functions in all areas of life. Catholic newspapers and periodicals are available to them; they are well informed. And, finally, the result of empirical experience, they have a keen sense of responsibility.

Following the unsuccessful 1863 uprising against Russia, enlightened Polish circles appealed to the nation to abandon temporarily dreams of political liberation through force and to commence *praca organiczna,* organic work. They asked their countrymen to fight illiteracy, to educate new cadres of engineers, technicians, and intellectuals of every kind.

In 1983 Poland is once again in political shambles, once again in thrall to Russian imperialist interests. And once again the Poles have the western world's sympathy—and that is about all. No western nation is about to cancel a single profitable contract for the sake of "their freedom and ours." There is a need to commence a new phase of organic work in order to preserve the substance of the Polish nation: to save and reinforce its national culture, to further its economic development, and to assure freedom of conscience and religious practice. Cooperation, yes. Collaboration, no.

How can this be accomplished? There are no clear and carefully worked out formulas. The pope's trip could have been helpful in this respect but it does not seem that these considerations ranked high on the agenda of the bishops who took part in preparing for the pope's trip. The bishops rested satisfied with the people's response to the pope, delighted with the surge of religiosity.

The courageous and vibrant faith of the Polish nation must mean that henceforth Polish Catholicism shall remain a perennial category in the life of the universal church. It also suggests that the means and methods which the Polish church finds for its relationships with society and its socialist rulers should serve as paradigms for serious study and research.

There is thus a common denominator between John Paul's first and second pilgrimages: the strengthening of popular Catholicism and the mandate to develop a new working relationship between politics and religion. Even John XXIII and the Fathers of Vatican II did not forsee an historical development of the type John Paul is pointing to.

Looking back on the Pope's June 1983 trip, two things emerge. First, the Soviet Union has, since 1956, resigned from its ideological offensive, its attempt to *persuade* the West, resorting instead to a display of military power. The Soviet leadership view themselves as governing a world empire and are not concerned about questions of public image. Second, the task of organic work, of developing cadres of devoted, thoughtful patriots who will cooperate without collaborating—this task remains of pivotal importance for the foreseeable future.

ART FOR POLITICS' SAKE
GETS SHELTERED UNDERGROUND[4]

Since the crushing of Solidarity by martial law—the war, it is always called here—many of Poland's writers, actors, artists and other intellectuals have gone into "internal emigration." They refuse to produce their work for the official market. Instead, they are channeling their talents into an emerging underground cultural life, which ranges from art exhibits held out of briefcases to thriving clandestine publishing houses issuing popular books and scholarly journals.

At the center of this ferment in recent months has been the Roman Catholic Church. Priests and parishioners have quietly organized programs on "Christian culture" that include political lectures by writers, historians, sociologists and former Solidarity union activists, meetings that resemble the underground "flying universities" of the late 1970's in Poland.

In a Warsaw church, for example, workers from the Huta Warszawa steel mill and the Nowotki electric motor factory recently listened to a psychiatrist speak on negotiating techniques and then asked him questions about the mistakes Solidarity made in its talks with the Government. Favorite themes besides Solidarity's rise and fall—it was outlawed under martial law on Dec. 13, 1981—include the current economic crisis and the history of the 19th century occupation of Poland by Czarist Russia, with emphasis on the failed uprising of 1863. "We read patriotic poems" was the way one priest put it.

The Catholic Church in Poland has traditionally been the refuge of patriotism in hard times. Since martial law, many churches have been decked with symbols of the outlawed union, including, in St. Bridget's church near the Gdansk shipyards, a portrait of the revered icon of the Black Madonna of Czestochowa wearing a Solidarity T-shirt. A weeklong cultural program in 15 churches

[4]Reprint of an article by John Kifner, correspondent. *New York Times.* p E5. F. 26, '84. Copyright © 1984 by The New York Times Company. Reprinted by permission.

in Wroclaw last November appears to have touched off the underground movement by dissident intellectuals, which is spreading
throughout the country. "It is an authentic explosion," said a former Solidarity leader from Silesia. "The cultural life has moved
from the open, official level to the welcoming doors of the church."
Added a Western diplomat: "They have an infrastructure in place,
and it's spreading so fast we can't keep up with it."

The efforts have drawn the unwelcome attention of the authorities and received a blow with an order from the primate,
Jozef Cardinal Glemp, for the transfer of an outspoken Solidarity
supporter, the Rev. Mieczyslaw Nowak, from his post in the
working-class suburb of Ursus to a rural parish. Father Nowak
was one of 69 activist priests who the Government last fall told
the church it wanted silenced, and Cardinal Glemp's critics
charged he was knuckling under.

In an unprecedented challenge to the primate's authority,
thousands of parishioners last week [February 1984] held nightly
protest masses, hooting down a representative from the church hierarchy who claimed the priest's transfer was a promotion. They
planned further actions when Cardinal Glemp returns in early
March from a trip to Latin America. In São Paulo, the primate
was quoted as saying that some elements of the church had ties
to Solidarity, "but I have chosen a more difficult and just approach, which is the pastoral path."

A year ago, Cardinal Glemp came under fire for urging actors
who were boycotting Polish television to go back to work. His suggestion was largely ignored. Instead, actors have channeled their
talents into the intellectual underground's "flying theaters," giving
clandestine shows at small gatherings around Warsaw.

After finishing their performance the other night at the State
Theater, for example, three actors rushed off to a private apartment, where about 50 people waited with chairs and mattresses
spread out around an open area that would serve as a stage. The
actors huddled together for a few moments, sipping glasses of
wine, working themselves into a new mood. Then they stepped
into the spotlights, improvised from reading lamps.

Skits From the Underground

Their performance was fast paced, professional and political. It was a revue of songs, skits and dramatic readings that shifted from ribald humor to chilling references to Poland's history of brutal occupations by foreign powers. The text ran from Polish leader Wojciech Jaruzelski's speech announcing the imposition of martial law to the topical lyrics of the cabaret artist Jan Pietrzak and the self-exiled protest singer Jacek Kaczmarski, with plenty of spoofs on the official press and television.

In one sketch, Little Red Riding Hood is carrying underground leaflets in her basket when she is accosted by two club-wielding wolves dressed as riot police; squirrels and sparrrows race ahead to Grandmother's house to warn her to hide the printing press.

In another, an old woman huddles in her apartment in fear because a Communist Party member has fallen to his death in a drunken stupor from an upstairs window. She is afraid it will be judged a murder and her neighbors will be rounded up and shot in retaliation, one of several references to the still searing memory of the Nazi occupation. Finally, she gathers her courage to write an anonymous letter to a newspaper advice column. "Don't worry, madam," came the reply. "This is a law-abiding country. Executions will be carried out only according to the following priorities: first, social parasites, second, pensioners, then students and schoolchildren." "Hey, that's not funny," a prominent lawyer in the audience shouted indignantly. The actors dissolved in laughter.

IN POLAND, A DIVIDED COMMUNIST PARTY
DEBATES HOW TO MAKE ITS IDEOLOGY WORK[5]

Poland's communists are taking a hard look at their party, and
they don't like what they see.

"Socialism is losing its ideological legitimacy," mourns Stanislaw Rainko, a member of the Institute of Basic Problems of Marxist-Leninism in Warsaw.

"It's disastrous," says Andrzej Burda, a university professor
in Lubin, a city in eastern Poland. Polish society, he asserts, "is
clearly indifferent" to socialism.

These harsh judgments are unusual enough in Poland. But
what is most surprising is that they appeared recently in the official journal of the Polish communist party, Nowe Dragi, or New
Roads. The fact that any criticism of Polish affairs could be printed in an official organ indicates the extent of the ideological turmoil within the party, known officially as the Polish United
Workers Party.

The party ideologues whose comments were solicited by Nowe
Dragi aren't questioning the future of communism. Rather, they
are calling for a new determination to make it work. Yet with the
party embroiled in factional infighting, Polish officials are finding
it difficult to do anything more than hold onto power.

"They can agree on the diagnosis, but not on the cure" to the
party's problems, one source close to the party says.

The current power struggle within the party involves several
factions. Hardliners want to eliminate ideological strays, while
moderates prefer more tolerance. Civilian officials, meanwhile,
are bristling at the growing authority being assumed by military
leaders in the government. The outcome of this battle for party
control will help shape Poland's future.

The party is still reeling from the presence of two other powerful political forces in Poland: the Solidarity labor movement, since

[5]Reprint of an article by Victoria Pope, special correspondent. Wall Street Journal. 203:35. F. 1, '84.
Reprinted by permission of the Wall Street Journal. Copyright © Dow Jones & Company, Inc. 1984. All
rights reserved.

banned, and the Roman Catholic Church. Pope John Paul II's visit to Poland last June [1983] had a particularly divisive effect on the party.

"I meet comrades who were good comrades years ago, and today they were moved by the visit of the pope," Mr. Burda complains in his article in Nowe Dragi. "Surely from people in the party you shouldn't expect emotions over the visit."

Adds Jerzy Ladyka of the Institute on Basic Problems of Marxist-Leninism: "The teachings of Pope John Paul II during the visit deepened and will continue to deepen deposits of irrationalism in the thinking of Poles."

Although Solidarity remains a potent political force, Polish officials may have been heartened by the relative calm that greeted this week's average 10% increase in the prices of some basic foods. Several hundred Solidarity supporters demonstrated Monday in Wroclaw, an industrial town in the southwest, but the group disbanded as soon as police appeared, officials said.

Although there were no reports of street demonstrations yesterday, riot police were deployed in Wroclaw, Gdansk and other Solidarity strongholds as a precautionary measure.

The government has been moving cautiously on food-price increases because they have provoked violent public reaction and were responsible for the labor revolt in July 1980 that sparked the Solidarity movement.

Solidarity's emergence caused a major upheaval in the party's ranks and seriously undercut its power base. Tens of thousands of party members left or were expelled for incompetence because of pressure from the labor union. Then, when the government cracked down on Solidarity and imposed martial law two years ago, many party members favoring change left or were forced out because their unorthodox views weren't any longer welcomed.

The upheaval isn't over. The party recently announced that some 8,000 members have been expelled since October as part of a drive to spruce up the membership. At the same time, the party enlisted 3,000 new members who presumably adhered more closely to the ideological line.

Overall, party membership has shrunk to only 2.2 million, or about 12% of the adult working population, from more than three million before the rise of Solidarity.

The party is split by more than ideological differences. Poland's leader, Gen. Wojciech Jaruzelski, has recently enhanced the military's role in his government, perhaps because he also detects weaknesses in the party ranks. Government insiders say Gen. Jaruzelski considers the army more trustworthy and disciplined than party bureaucrats. In the past two years, several career military officers have been appointed to posts formerly held by civilian party members.

Yet the declining popularity of the party, and socialism, appears to be the major worry. Several ideologues who appeared in Nowe Dragi blamed antigovernment teachers for poisoning students' minds and turning them against communism at an early age. And some party hardliners are calling for further expulsions from the party, especially those members suspected of sympathizing with the Roman Catholic Church.

The ideological divisions within the Communist Party aren't likely to be resolved soon.

POLAND: STILL DEFIANT[6]

Dusk, with a steady, bone-chilling drizzle. An abandoned concrete watchtower sits at one end of the bridge. The car slowly dodges the potholes.

The span over the Oder is ugly and dilapidated. Neither the East Germans on one side nor the Poles on the other side would dream of repairing it, a sign of their mutual disdain. The river below is a thin brown stream, disappointing, considering the bloody course it has wended through history.

The East German guardhouse squats on the other side technically on Polish ground. Eric Ambler would love it here. The reek of black tobacco, the hard stares at the passport held under the gooseneck lamp, the inquisitions, the rubber stamp pounded down with an executioner's swing.

[6]Reprint of an article by John Darnton, Bureau Chief of the *New York Times* in Warsaw and winner of the Pulitzer Prize in 1982 for his reporting. *New York Times Magazine.* p 24–9+. Ag. 22, '82. Copyright © 1982 by The New York Times Company. Reprinted by permission.

But the waiting is nerve-racking, hours and hours behind the drone of windshield wipers. The East Germans are being relentless. Car panels torn out; body searches. The guards hold up each piece of paper and read it, sometimes upside down. This is strange, for it is February 1982 and Poland, plunged into martial law, is supposedly once again a reliable "fraternal" nation. The Poles returning from visits abroad look nervous. They are bringing in coffee, soap, meat wrapped in plastic bags that bleed on the wet pavement. Many, you are sure, are smuggling in gold, clothes to sell, zlotys purchased in West Berlin at one-tenth the official rate. There are guns everywhere; officials moving with abrupt darting motions; a pervasive sense of fear.

And then, incredibly, it is over. The road beyond is deserted and dips around a bend into a forest. It is dark.

Half a mile ahead, five men in Polish Army uniforms step out of the bushes. Their bayonets gleam in the headlights. The commander flags you down ferociously. He leans against the roof, demands to know your nationality, where you are coming from.

Then he reaches into his pocket. He thrusts something through the window. It is an old, crumpled French note, 100 francs. "I was wondering ," he says, "if you would be good enough to exchange this for dollars. I'll give you a good rate."

You have left behind the Oder, the efficiency, the stares, and you are back in Poland, the same old inscrutable, confused, troublemaking, muddling-through Poland, martial law or no martial law.

It is also the third Poland I have seen in my nearly three years here. First, there was the Poland of Edward Gierek, the former party chairman, with his ambitious development schemes, who is now in disgrace. That was a time of cynicism, apathy and pretense—and of prosperity disappearing before everyone's eyes like milk down a drain. Then there was the Poland of Solidarity and Lech Walesa. It was a time when horizons suddenly opened up, the blinkers came off, and there was hope of creating a livable, productive, nonschizophrenic society within the Soviet bloc. And now the Poland of Gen. Wojciech Jaruzelski, a Poland of tanks and underground leaflets, where the structures of control are in place, but just barely—a crumbling facade with a scaffold around it. In this new Poland, the fear and the dream commingle and everyone waits for something to happen—*something*. . . .

August 1979

Confusing—this moonscape. On our first day in Poland, my wife, Nina, and I dine at Bazyliszek, the one luxury restaurant in the Old Town section of Warsaw. An atmosphere of faded Viennese elegance, with crystal chandeliers, brass samovars, wild boar on the menu and a string quartet in the corner playing Mozart. Outside, on the cobblestones of Market Square, sits a young woman with straight blond hair, a gold star pasted under one eye and a guitar. She sings an old Dave Van Ronk song in strangely accented English. The words rise up, distinct between the spaces in the Mozart: "Baby, you been away *too-o-o long.*"

The Old Town is, for my money, the most magnificent nub of any city in the world. In Nuremberg, Cracow and Prague, the medieval buildings totter and list with authentic age. Here they are as neat as picket-fence slats, instant Gothic, dating from the 1950s, when the Government decided to rebuild the heaping ruins of the Nazi-occupation era brick by brick. Crafts that had died out a century ago were revived; old Canaletto paintings were copied to re-create the archways, gutters and gargoyles.

Later, I drive by the sprawling housing developments on the outskirts of Warsaw. Huge concrete slabs are scattered about like giant cinder blocks, monotonous in design and appalling in their cheap regard for living space. The priorities sink in: the sense of a golden, royal past, a desperate attempt to climb backward in time, and a gray future that crawls ahead without a vision of what shall be or should be. I have been here three weeks and I have yet to meet a self-professed Communist.

But, house-hunting, I discover the moneyed operators. In the exclusive Mokotow section, I came up against the same landlord four times. It is illegal in Poland to own more than one house. He feels compelled to explain. One house belongs to his wife; another, to his sister; a third, to his son. His son, I learn later, is in primary school.

The landlord shows me an upstairs bedroom. Its window has been bricked down to the size of an envelope. Regulations, he explains: This way, it's only a storage room. In the living room, metal rods hang down from the ceiling, so low that we have to stoop. Technically, he has reduced the room's dimensions so that it's not a room at all. Don't worry, he assures me, the rods will come down as soon as the inspectors come and go.

The rent for the house, officially set at 9,000 zlotys ($300) a month, will be paid to the state, but he wants five times that sum for himself, in dollars, under the table. Also, to reduce the Government's take, he proposes that we say we are sharing the house. He begins to pace off "his" half of the kitchen. I protest. The deal falls through. I hear him mutter, "Idiot. Doesn't know what country he's in."

September 1979

An official guide is showing me around. He seems a bit defensive about my interest in the 500,000 Jews who lived in Warsaw before the Holocaust. He shows me where the tracks were of the trains that took them off to Treblinka. The raised foundations of earth under the high-rise apartments of the former ghetto still contain human bones. The monument to the heroes of the ghetto uprising is built with the very same granite that Hitler had planned to use to commemorate the liquidation of Poland's Jews. The monument is impressive. But it is the only one in Warsaw without flowers.

The guide then takes me to a church. He guides me steathily down an aisle to plaques on the wall in memory of the war dead. Lists and list of names, town, dates. Finally one name leaps out: "Katyn."

"The date, the date, look at the date," whispers the guide.

I see the year 1940. I realize he is telling me the church believes that the Katyn Forest massacres of an estimated 15,000 Polish prisoners of war took place at a time when the area was in Soviet hands—that it was Stalin's work, not Hitler's, as Moscow claims. And the deeper meaning that this is the agony of Eastern Europe, where Germans kill Jews and Russians kill Poles, where the flagstones are steeped in blood, and where thousands can slip into graves unnoticed by history.

The next day, I go into a furniture store to buy a chair.

"Nie ma" ("There are none"), says the saleswoman, barely looking up from her newspaper.

But how about all those chairs in the window?

"Dekoracja" ("Decoration"), she says, mumbling something to herself. I think I hear that word again: "Idiot."

November 1979

The town of Czechowice-Dziedzice, in the mining region of Silesia. A flat landscape of blackened smokestacks, dirty red-brick buildings and concrete high-rises, with an occasional clump of sad, scraggly pines. There has been an explosion at a mine. Two men are dead and 20 are trapped in a tunnel 600 feet underground, where a methane-gas fire is still raging.

It is the third mine disaster in the past month; in all, some 43 lives have been lost. The accidents coincide with a new brigade system that keeps the mines going 24 hours a day, seven days a week. The Government is desperate for foreign exchange; it is squeezing the miners for more and more of its "black gold."

Appointments with officials at the mine are made for me at the Mining Ministry office in Katowice, 32 miles away; they send me off with handshakes. I arrive at Czechowice-Dziedzice and something has gone wrong. The official has been called away, the gate is locked. I bounce back and forth for two days. A local party secretary finally loses patience and tells me to get the hell out of town. My car is followed by a Polonez, the favored model of the U.B., the secret police.

My translator and I find a small bar named Barborka, after St. Barbara, the patron saint of miners. We enter a smoky cavern smelling of beer and sweat, and the bawl of conversation stops. Hostile eyes rimmed with coal dust turn to the stranger in a necktie. No one moves to ease our path to the bar.

Two beers later, my translator explains to the nearest table that I am an American journalist who has read about the mine disaster and has come to see what happened. A miner lurches up; his face is three inches from my own.

"First thing," he says, "you've got to realize that all the papers in this country are crap—crap and lies."

"They're scared of the truth and they're scared of us," says his companion. "And, by Christ, the Government better do something and do it fast, or we'll do something ourselves."

There follows, over the next hour, an unremitting stream of complaints, threats and curses, despite the presence of a shadow who creeps in and sits down nearby. Rarely have I encountered such burning anger, a pure, white-hot, we're-going-to-get-the-bastards anger. And these are the miners, the elite of the Polish work force, coddled with special meat shops and goods unavailable to others. These are the men who refused to join in the anti-Government upheavals of 1956, 1970 and 1976.

We toast cousins in Chicago. Leaving, I see the Polonez sitting empty down the street.

The next morning, I return to the mine. The party secretary tells me I got his workers drunk to elicit the kind of information spies are interested in.

And the fire in the mine? "None of your business," he says. "And don't you worry. Everything here is under control."

Three days later, they bring up the dead bodies.

August 1980

When the revolt comes, it is deeper and more disciplined than anyone expected. At the Lenin shipyard in Gdansk, the strikers' faces are dirt-streaked but radiant, solemn and lighthearted at the same time. The workers lounge about on the grass, listening to their leaders on loudspeakers, and, on transistor radios, to the BBC, Voice of America and Radio Free Europe. They marvel at the speed of news when it flows freely; they can take a vote and hear it come back over the little box within the hour.

The hall swarms with delegates from other factories joining the strike. A life-size plaster statue of Lenin gazes reflectively into the distance. To my surprise, I am given a seat on the raised stage of the strike committee. The delegates sit at long tables, as at a banquet—dockworkers, shipbuilders, tool-die machinists, assembly-line workers, bus drivers. Some write the names of their factories on placards as if they were attending a Rotarian convention.

More strikes are announced. Somewhere in the list, after an electrical factory in Elblag, I hear: "The New York Times." A cheer goes up. With everyone expecting an attack by armed troops, the foreign press seems to offer a glimmer of protection. At least, the world will know.

Food is brought to the locked gate by well-wishers. Overhead, a plane drops leaflets proclaiming the strike over.

Lech Walesa is rushing around, bobbing his head in hurried conferences, giving orders, grabbing the microphone to calm the workers with joking patter. Only a month ago, he was an unknown, unemployed activist for the minuscule Baltic Coast Free Trade Union. I talk to Anna Walentynowicz, the 50-year-old crane operator whose dismissal sparked the strike. She describes the agony of 1970, when workers were shot down. She got into trouble later for passing a hat to buy flowers to their memory. This time, it will be different, she says. No more marching through the streets; stay close to the machines and wait. I ask her for her political views. "I'm a democrat," she says. "But mostly, I believe in God."

August 26, 1980

The strikes are still on. Stefan Cardinal Wyszynski, the Primate of Poland, delivers a sermon that is actually broadcast over state television. A group of workers in the Gdynia shipyard are huddled in a room, hanging on his every word. He is their spiritual monarch, for 30 years the only authority they have respected. (Cardinal Wyszynski died in May 1981.)

Cardinal Wyszynski calls for peace, calm, reason, respect. True, he criticizes the Government, but he warns that strikes could pose a threat to the nation; he pleads for workers to be patient and postpone some of their demands. He refers to the partitions of Poland: "Let us remember with what difficulty we regained our freedom after 125 years." All this mixed in with religious metaphors honed to perfection from his decades of slipping elliptical meanings past the Communist authorities.

The speech is of critical importance. The church, in so many words, has told the workers to stop. What effect will it have?

The room is silent. A strike leader strides to the front and flips off the television. "Friends," he says, "as we have just heard, the Primate supports us right down the line."

A roar of applause and cheers. I learn, at that moment, a fundamental truth about the Roman Catholic Church in Poland. It resides so deeply in the people's hearts, in those recesses of nationalism and legend, that it can never be uprooted. When its words come into conflict with its own image, they are not ignored, they are magically transposed. The image is stronger; it is, in a sense, the real church.

Five days later, Solidarity is born.

October 1980

The country is opening up—a headlong tide. New groups are forming. Liberals, reformers, even radicals, are taking over institutions, such as the journalists' union, that have been instruments of party control. Yet all this is unfolding peacefully, methodically, even democratically. It all seems part of what Jacek Kuron, the brilliant, barrel-chested long-time dissident, calls a "self-limiting revolution." The idea is to turn the authorities upside down without overthrowing them; to transform Poland without disturbing the geopolitical balance and bringing in the Russians. It is a tricky business.

Newspapers, incredibly, are printing news. I am having tea at the house of a friend, a former Polish ambassador, when a political activist arrives. Breathlessly, he pulls a typewritten document from his coat lining and says conspiratorially, "Have you seen the latest demands?"

My host answers graciously, "Thank you, I have. They're in today's newspapers."

Even the security apparatus seems a bit more human. Janusz Onyszkiewicz, Solidarity's national spokesman, is on the telephone talking to a friend in London about whether a Polish exile should return. "Tell him it's safe." Onyszkiewicz says.

"I don't know," says the friend.

"Tell him everything's changed now," says Onyszkiewicz.

"I'm not sure."

A third voice cuts into the line. "For God's sake, tell him *we* say it's O.K."

November 1980

I go to a political cabaret. There is a curious mix in the audience, dissident intellectuals seated across the room from party and Government officials. But one central table up front is empty until the final moment. When it fills, there is a stir; eyes turn, waiters rush to push in chairs; people drift by, hoping for a nod of recognition. The latecomers are steel-mill workers and Solidarity activists. They are the new celebrities.

Something of a social revolution is under way. It is consummate paradox to feel the winds of class warfare in a Communist state. It is as if all those statues of "worker heroes" had suddenly come alive.

The party is widely seen as the agent of exploitation. People are leaving it in droves. Across the country, workers strike to back up demands that hospitals, clinics, rest homes and vacation spas reserved for the police and party elite be given to "the people." Fancy cars left on the streets overnight are likely to have their windshields smashed.

At the Ursus tractor factory outside Warsaw, thousands gather in the movie hall to prepare for a strike. The issue is the "Narozniak affair," the arrest of a Solidarity volunteer for disseminating a classified state document. Tempers are rising. A lanky political dissident gives advice on how to stand up under police interrogation. Another reads a poem about the glory of dying for Poland; it sends shudders of excitement through the hall. One young man grips the mike earnestly and begins with a gaffe—"Comrades," he calls out. Twitters and chuckles. He blushes deeply and recovers, but two minutes later he slips again—"Another thing we should remember, comrades. . . ." This time there are howls of laughter. Flustered and red-faced, he can only sit down. Party membership has become a scarlet letter.

December 1980

Things are moving fast. Films previously banned by the censor are playing on television. Universities are preparing to choose their own rectors by democratic elections. Parliament is becoming fractious. There is a kind of national euphoria; the whole country resembles a university coffeehouse plunged into frenetic discussions about unions, socialism, society. It seems that no meeting can adjourn before 3 in the morning.

Passports for travel abroad are available almost for the asking. It's as if the world has suddenly opened up. No matter that the neighboring "fraternal" countries have sealed their borders: Who wants to go *there?* Poles are coming back from the West to sniff the breezes—writers and scholars who left in official disgrace in 1968, émigrés who had vowed never to set foot in the country again.

New Year's Eve is a frenzied round of parties. The toasts become more and more outrageous, the champagne spills onto the floor. Men kiss each other on the cheek, women hug each other and exchange wishes in intimate tones. Jan, my sardonic friend, raises his glass and says: "And to you, as a journalist, I wish a Soviet invasion." Our friends laugh. It is too unthinkable.

Walking home in the middle of the street, we meet other groups of revelers. Beautiful Ania, who had looked so drawn and sad in the picture taken years before for a passport that never came, sighs and breathes deeply of the dank air. She opens her arms, as though to the night, and says: "All my life I've wanted to live in a free country. And now, just to think, my own country is becoming free."

January 1981

Breakfast with Lech Walesa at the Solec Hotel, a sort of rundown Polish version of a Holiday Inn. Two busloads of Soviet tourists pull up. They enter—bulky, chattering, the big-bosomed women, the men in their crinkly suits. How will they react when they see Walesa, the devil incarnate, the man threatening to bring down their empire?

They sit down. They order breakfast as if they own the place. They eat. Nothing happens. Of course they know the name, but not the face: He is so dangerous that they've never been shown a picture of him.

I look at Walesa and I realize that I know the face but not the man. How many times have I interviewed him? Maybe 10 or 15. How many times have I seen him sitting in his office, presiding at meetings, speaking to crowds? Maybe 30 or 40. And yet he remains elusive.

He has become such an international superstar there seems to be little left over. The legend of Walesa as dyed-in-the-wool worker, church-goer, folk hero is beginning to overshadow the man. He is, without doubt, a gifted leader—courageous, instinctive, articulate. But there is a darker side to his nature—his dictatorial tendencies, his pettiness, his intolerance. These traits have been coming to the fore, affecting his leadership. Some of his top lieutenants are becoming disenchanted; the movement is in danger of splitting.

Walesa repeatedly says that it is unity—millions of unarmed workers standing shoulder to shoulder against the state—that has made Solidarity into what it is. If that goes, the union is lost.

February 1981

The Tomb of the Unknown Soldier in Warsaw's Victory Square. The tomb, containing the ashes of a Polish soldier who died in the fighting that repelled a Soviet invasion in 1920, has become a rallying point for all kinds of demonstrations. It is guarded at all times by four Polish soldiers standing erect and immobile. Every few hours, they are replaced by four others, who goose-step from a garrison acrosss the square. On this day, Rural Solidarity, the new independent farmers' union, has been refused legal status by the courts. The farmers, large men with calloused hands, whose Sunday suits are rumpled from all-night bus trips, are confused and angry. They march to the tomb.

The crowd grows; there are thousands. Speeches start up. Tough, defiant words are shouted. Suddenly, from across the square, come the guards. They march straight for the tomb, right toward the crowd—they have no choice. They get closer, 10 feet away, five feet.

Suddenly, the crowd parts, an aisle opens up, and, as the soldiers march through, a chant rises: "Long live the Polish Army!" "God bless the army!"

The soldiers take their places. I look at one of them. He is ramrod stiff and expressionless. But tears flow down his cheeks.

March 1981

The lines in front of the stores seem endless. They practically merge into each other. The huddled, shivering figures conjure up visions of revolution and turmoil. In reality, the country is remarkably quiet, even subdued. The shortages are so bad that conspiracy theories develop. The Government, it is rumored, is intentionally holding goods off the market to blacken Solidarity. One writer tells his tablemates he has it on good authority that the goods are being stored in a secret tunnel constructed by the Nazis during the occupation. It's hard to tell if he's joking.

The strikes continue sporadically. They sound worse when they are read about outside the country, making it seem that the whole place is swirling in a vortex. But many of the strikes are local affairs, undertaken to oust a local administrator, or to get a police building converted to a clinic, or just to test muscle. I suspect they're not as detrimental to the economy as the Government makes out. I'm at one factory when a one-hour strike ends. The workers move dutifully over to the assembly line, but the conveyor belt doesn't move. "We don't have any parts, anyway," one worker explains.

But the economy, strapped for foreign exchange because of Gierek's live-now, pay-later borrowing policy, is in a state of collapse. A group of farmers from the south persuade the Solidarity chapter at the Ursus factory to build tractors for them on weekends. They go to another chapter and borrow the money, which is to be repaid with potatoes and cabbage. It's the only way to get anything done: Bypass the state altogether.

Mismanagement and inefficiency are rife. Goods are shipped to the wrong places, essential parts are missing, things are ordered and don't arrive. Cigarettes almost run out because there is no glue. Writers, who are guaranteed an allotment of paper, are composing novels on the backs of rejected manuscripts. I hear of a chocolate factory where no chocolates are being produced because there is no paper to wrap them in. But everyone goes to work, punching the time clock in and out.

December 1981

Back in August 1980, our maid Kasia Trzcinska, suggested matter-of-factly that I should meet her son, Jurek. I put her off. A few weeks later, she raised the subject again. I explained that I would love to meet her son and her whole family, but that I was up to my neck trying to write about Solidarity and all the changes shaking Poland.

Not long after that, her son telephoned. "I'm coming to Warsaw tomorrow," he announced.

"Good," I said, not very enthusiastically.

"I'll be driving down with some other people," he said. "Lech Walesa, Bogdan Lis, a few others. You see, we have this new union we're trying to get registered."

Jurek Trzcinski, it turned out, was a top Solidarity leader. A large man with a rakish mustache, he had a bemused expression that he put on to parry my queries about Soviet intervention. From Jurek I derived my respect for the integrity, courage and basic level-headedness of the Polish working class. Night after night, he explained the goals—not to drag Poland out of the Warsaw Pact, not to overthrow the state, but to set things right. "We just want a decent country," he would say.

Jurek often visited us with Bogdan Lis, Walesa's right-hand man. One day, they came from a meeting with striking farmers. Lis pinned a new button, a green Solidarity badge, on the lapel of my youngest daughter, 7-year old Liza. She stood straight, eyes wide and solemn.

"Do you know about Solidarity?" Lis asked her

"Yes," she replied.

"And what is it?" he prodded.

"Solidarity wants to make the Polish people free."

With a whoop of pleasure, he hugged her and spun her into the air.

For some reason, that scene flashed through my mind when my phone and telex went dead at 11:10 on the night of Dec. 12, 1981, and I drove through the streets to file a story and encountered police vans closing off both ends of the block where Solidarity's Warsaw headquarters is located.

December 13, 1981

Martial law came down like a sledgehammer. It caught everybody off guard. Solidarity's leaders, who had arrived at Gdansk for a general meeting, were brought meekly down the stairwells of their hotels, their hands behind their backs. Many of our friends were dragged out of bed, some not even given time to put on their shoes. When Walesa was seized at his Gdansk apartment in the early hours of Dec. 13 and flown to Warsaw, he was convinced, reliable sources told me later, that he was going to be thrown out of the plane.

Jurek evaded arrest and went into hiding. But shortly afterward, four policemen with a dog came to his apartment for his wife. She shouted at them: "Criminals, bandits! I will not go with you—you'll have to shoot me right here." Her 8-year-old daughter screamed, "Mama!" and her 87-year-old mother threw herself at a policeman's feet, begging them to leave her daughter alone. But they arrested Jurek's wife and dragged her away.

One reason the military takeover came as such a surprise sounds a bit ludicrous in retrospect. There was no provision in the Polish Constitution for a state of emergency; a bill that would allow for one was being prepared for Parliament. Until the bill passed, the thinking ran, a military crackdown couldn't happen. So great was the illusion that democracy had already taken root that it was difficult to imagine the authorities acting illegally.

The key to the operation was isolation. The whole nation was cut off from the rest of the world and plunged into a blackout. All communications were severed, all travel banned, all meetings prohibited. Every household was isolated from every other, every factory, every division within a factory. The power of the union lay in numbers and concerted action, which depended on communication, openness and visibility. Once these were blotted out with curfews, roadblocks, dead telephones and jammed radio broadcasts, the power dissipated.

The generals did more than arrest 6,000 Solidarity leaders and supporters. Figuratively, they place the entire population under arrest.

December 27, 1981

I climb the stairs to the third-floor apartment of an old friend, a journalist and writer who loved to exchange theories and gossip over the kitchen table. He opens the door a crack, peers out and steps onto the landing.

"I can't see you," he says. "They just hauled me in. I was warned not to talk to any foreigners."

His eyes are dark circles. I have never seen them like that before.

The first week of martial law, it snowed heavily. The snow is a metaphor for the stillness and deadness that have descended upon the land. There are strikes, but they are broken up brutally by army tanks and the ZOMO, the dreaded paramilitary police in their camouflage uniforms. At two mines in Silesia, miners stay underground for weeks, convinced that the entire country is on strike. Only when their wives tell them this is not true do they give up and come to the surface, defeated and bitter.

I go to the Huta Warszawa steel mill the morning after a strike there has been broken. About 100 workers cluster about the front gate. They describe how their factory was surrounded by tanks, how the strike leaders were isolated in one part of the plant and the women started crying and fear set in. "We gave up without a struggle," says one man, still disbelieving.

As we are talking, a man in a cloth overcoat comes over and loudly demands to see my identification. The crowd turns on him. "Let's lynch the bastard," someone shouts.

Another man, in a fine imported suede coat, sidles up and politely but firmly orders me to leave.

January 1982

For Western journalists, accustomed to freedoms of news coverage unthinkable in the rest of the Soviet bloc, it is as if a tight net has been drawn around the country overnight. Borders are sealed to all but a departing trickle of foreigners. Telexes and telephones are dead. Within days, heavy-handed censorship is instituted.

We are followed and at times harrassed. My Volvo begins getting flat tires from nails, screws and sharpened belt buckles. A television series called "Who Is Who?" centers on three American diplomats who are called spies; the aim is to cut contacts between Poles and foreigners. The police spread the word that anyone passing petitions or information to Western journalists is liable to be charged with treason and could draw a 15-year prison sentence.

Remarkably, none of my contacts—whose who are still at liberty—drop away. But our meetings are fraught with cloak-and-dagger intrigue. We arrange to bump into each other at public locations, in front of a certain picture at the National Museum or in front of a certain post-office box. They slip me notes and underground bulletins. A hiding place is arranged for further written communication.

Every two days, I meet with an especially valuable source, a young man I'll call Karol. We set up an elaborate system of rendezvous points, mostly coffeehouses in the Old Town; if he is not at one, I am to go on to another. I notice that he is almost always a few minutes late. Before he comes, a young woman enters, surveys the room inconspicuously and leaves, barely glancing in my direction.

During one of our talks, I mention the risk he is running and ask him why he is doing it. "Must have been all those movies I saw in my youth about the resistance," he jokes. Like him, I feel as if I'm in a movie most of my waking hours.

The journalists' major preoccupation is getting the story out. There is a single secret channel available once a day. We use it for a pooled dispatch, which goes to every newspaper and radio station in the United States that asks for it. Slipping other stories past border guards strains ingenuity, especially since the authorities begin strip-searching suspicious-looking passengers at the airport. Somehow, one young man walks through with stories stuffed into both of his boots.

One of my stories gets out on a ferry to Sweden. Another is slipped under a cushion in a railroad car that goes through East Germany. A third is stuffed into the bottom of a Marlboro cigarette pack that is then resealed. There is no way of knowing which of them, if any, reaches New York.

Finally, I hit upon a sure-fire system. Because there are no facilities in Poland for developing color film, the Poles permit some photographers to send their film out undeveloped. The photographers are closely watched anyway, so the film is deemed safe. One of them photographs three of my stories; the undeveloped roll is passed by the censor and ends up in Bonn, where a lab technician, in developing the film, finds a message to pass the copy on to New York.

March 1982

Poles were proud of the alliance between intellectuals and workers in Solidarity, although differences between them remained. The differences are there under martial law, too. A friend, who is a writer and critic, was detained, and in his jail cell he met another detainee, a bus driver. They talked.

"Do you have any children?" asked the bus driver.

"Yes," the writer replied, "two small children."

"So do I. Were yours awake when they came for you?"

"Thank God, they were asleep."

"Yeah," said the bus driver. "Mine were sleeping too. But I woke them up. I wanted them to remember all their lives how those bastards came and took away their father."

The incident set the writer to thinking. Intellectuals, he concluded, were not "fierce" enough. "We think too much. Workers really know how to hate and how to pass that hatred on."

April 1982

Martial law has solved nothing, because the Government has done nothing. So far, it has moved neither to create a "national accord" nor to outlaw Solidarity outright. A Polish journalist compares the situation to "a patient slowly waking up after a powerful anesthetic and finding that no operation has taken place."

Others compare it to the Nazi occupation, even though it is clearly far from that. They seem to do this for effect, to indicate the depth of the anger and alienation from the regime. They talk of "the war" as shorthand for "state of war," the martial-law provision. It's a curious turn of phrase, lending a kind of melodrama to what was, when all is said and done, a military operation accomplished with little bloodshed. I wonder if it isn't a psychological crutch of sorts, a way of covering what some concede is their shame over the fact that there wasn't more resistance.

Curiously, regard for the army is still high. The hatred is heaped upon the ZOMO. With their reliability open to question, the conscripted army troops were given only backup tasks during strike-breaking and were quickly withdrawn whenever they fraternized with civilian workers. This does not augur well for a regime whose power now rests upon military might. The army's loyalty has not been tested fully, and how it would respond if things got worse and orders given to fire upon strikers or demonstrators is open to question. Government officials bristle when the word "junta" is used, but the military is dominant in the power structure and the party shows no signs of reviving.

Officials parrot the line that Poland was on the verge of civil war, that anarchy was threatening to suck it under, and that martial law was a last, desperate chance to save the nation. But they have difficulty mustering evidence to support these claims. Certainly there was no "anarchy" in the streets, in the sense of disorders, nor was there any sign of an opposition ready to take up arms. There was, on the other hand, widespread realization that the political situation was veering out of control and that Solidarity was again preparing to mount a challenge to the party.

This has led to the notion among some observers in the West that Solidarity brought on martial law by going "too far" in its demands. But it could also be argued that the party went back on the power-sharing arrangement struck in Gdansk in August 1980. Most of the 21 original demands of the Lenin shipyard strikers remained unfulfilled.

Faced with the party's intransigence, Solidarity's leadership adopted more radical stances and did battle over once-untouchable issues. But the extremists in the union never really gained control. And the union's actions had a way of ending up more moderate than its rhetoric.

At the end, the union tried—naively, it turned out—to bypass the Polish party altogether and address itself directly to Moscow. This was the significance of Solidarity's call, at its final meeting on Dec. 12, 1981, for a national referendum on membership in the Warsaw Pact. The union counted on a vote for continued membership; the idea was to convince Moscow that the military guarantee the Russians needed could be provided not just by the Polish party but by Polish society as a whole. The meeting was seized upon as the pretext for the crackdown, although Western military experts believe the move must have been planned much earlier, if only for logistical reasons.

All along, the great unknown was how much latitude the Soviet Union would allow. Clearly conscious of the costs of intervention, Moscow displayed a tolerance that surpassed the expectations of many in the West. What Moscow could not tolerate was any tampering with the Polish party's sacred "leading role." In the Kremlin's view, the party was the one and only reliable instrument of control; without it, both "socialism" and Soviet domination fell apart.

The inherent contradictions were insurmountable. A Communist Party with minority support was trying to pull an entire country away from the direction it wanted to go in. It was struggling with a new, popular rival. Anything that Moscow did to bolster or bully it only reinforced the conviction that it was the agent of alien rule. The "leading role" was a fiction whose time had come.

In retrospect, the critical turning point came in March 1981, when the union voted a nationwide general strike to protest police beatings in Bydgoszcz. That was a do-or-die moment, when the union's strength was at a peak, the resolve of the authorities shaky and Moscow's intentions unclear. A general strike, if won, might have forced the authorities into honest cooperation.

Instead, Walesa and a few other negotiators bypassed the union's democratic decision-making procedures to negotiate a last-minute settlement. This opened up fissures in the movement and strengthened hard-liners in the party. Union negotiators said afterward that the authorities had informed them that the Russians would invade if they did not give way. History may never know if that was true or not.

June 1982

Jurek, I learn, has been arrested. He has gone on trial in Gdynia with eight other defendants. They are charged with distributing antistate leaflets and fomenting a strike at a naval academy. The strike, such as it was, occurred at a time when classes were suspended, and it was quickly called off.

The trial is brief. Even relatives of the accused find it hard to get into the courtroom. Key defense witnesses are not allowed to speak. In his summation, the judge passes quickly over the charges and emphasizes that some of the accused were known Solidarity activists. The sentences are preordained and severe. Jurek is given nine years.

In prison, his head is shaved clean, his mustache is shaved off. His face swells up, apparently from poor diet. His mother weeps often, especially on warm sunny days, when she looks out the window and imagines her son in a dank cell.

Everyone is slumped in a moral depression. Journalists are being fired left and right. Universities are being purged. People direct their energies toward schemes to get out of the country. No one seems to be doing any work.

A campaign is under way to boycott the regime. Intellectuals and professionals withhold their services. One actor I know works as a waiter in a coffeehouse. A well-known singer is pumping gas. A woman television broadcaster in Wroclaw is selling ice cream at a small stand in the market square.

There is an occupation-regime atmosphere about everyday events. A soccer game between a Soviet team and a Polish one is held under tight security; ZOMO troops with automatic weapons ring the stadium; the stands are divided into quadrants by uniformed police. On flights of the Polish airline, a ZOMO with his hand on his AK-47 stands at the back of the cabin, on the lookout for hijackers.

On the other hand, there is a laxity and inconsistency to the crackdown that seems in keeping with the Polish character. One man I know who is in hiding comes up from time to time for a meal at his favorite restaurant. Another public figure in hiding, the former head of the journalists' association, is said to have received heart medication, through an intermediary, from an official in the Ministry of the Interior.

In Victory Square there is a huge cross, made entirely of flowers, lying on the flagstones. Twice the police have removed it, and each time it has been reconstituted, bigger than before. Near the cross is a small shrine to nine miners shot by the police at Wujek in December. One day, someone brought a marble plaque with the nine names engraved on it. The police removed it. The next day, there were nine lumps of coal. They, too, were removed. The next day, there were nine crucifixes. And so it goes.

Last month a British diplomat was walking across the square when he chanced to see a young man picked up by two ZOMO while kneeling beside the cross. The man did not resist as he was led away into a police van. Once inside, he was beaten savagely with nightsticks. The diplomat, peering through a window, counted 26 blows to the head and stomach before he was spotted and ordered to move on. He felt certain that the young man must have died.

Official thuggery is on the rise. On May 3, during pro-Solidarity demonstrations, policemen bashed heads all over the place. Clouds of tear gas billowed from one end of town to the other. Late in the evening, I went to meet someone at the train station. At an underground track, where there is a television set fixed to the wall, a crowd had gathered for the evening news. Four ZOMO were standing in the center, their nightsticks still bent and scuffed. Around them were young men, obviously demonstrators. Everyone was watching the clashes on the news—in effect, watching themselves.

That is the image of Poland I carry away with me—oppressor
and oppressed standing side by side, watching the theater of their
country's disintegration. I do not know what will happen here; no
one does. What everyone knows is that the conflict and the anguish are far from over. Perhaps next time the explosion will be
violent. There is not really much to tell Jurek's mother to comfort
her, except that there's a chance he will not serve his full nine
years, that something will happen before then.

POLISH REGIME TAKES ON THE CHURCH, AND REGRETS IT[7]

Sometimes it seems as if Poland's Communist regime is really
in cahoots with the anti-government underground when it comes
to causing social unrest.

Take, for example, the regime's latest display of shooting itself
in the foot—its decision to remove crucifixes and other religious
objects from schools, hospitals and other state institutions. The
move has touched off a fresh wave of restiveness in a nation that
can scarcely afford more domestic difficulties, and has prompted
another confrontation between the government and the Roman
Catholic Church that could easily have been avoided.

The regime's reason for ordering the removal of the religious
objects from state facilities seems plausible. As government
spokesman Jerzy Urban put it, "The state does not attempt to sec-
ularize the churches, and the churches should not attempt to cleri-
calize state institutions." The government cites the United States
and other Western democracies in support of its case.

But Poland is different from the Western democracies. It is
also different from the Soviet Union and every other East European state. And the key difference lies in the power and respect the
church enjoys among the people of a communist state. Nowhere

[7]Reprint of an article by Harry Trimborn, assistant foreign news editor. *Los Angeles Times.* p IV2.
Mar. 25, '84. Copyright © 1984 Los Angeles Times. Reprinted by permission.

in the communist world does religion, organized or otherwise, enjoy such privileges, power and prestige as it does in Poland.

The Polish church is far more than an edifice of faith for the nearly 80% of the nation's 36 million inhabitants who regularly attend its services. It is, as it has been throughout Poland's tragic history, the symbol and guardian of the country's national identity, its traditions and culture. This centuries-old link is what a priest involved in the latest controversy probably had in mind when he said, "There is no Poland without the cross."

And as the only national non-governmental institution, the church serves more than the spiritual needs of its followers. So it made little sense for the regime deliberately to provoke a confrontation with the church over a long-dormant issue that nobody—except perhaps some bureaucratic hardheads—had thought much about, and to do it by selecting Christendom's most revered symbol—the crucifix.

There was no need for the regime to act. The display of crucifixes and other religious objects in state classrooms and elsewhere resulted from no sudden anti-government provocation.

Crucifixes had been a fixture of the Stanislaw Staszic Agricultural College in Mietno, 40 miles southeast of Warsaw, since it opened in 1924. The communist governments of the postwar era had not seen fit to change the school's name. Stanislaw Staszic was a priest who had been minister of education before the partition of Poland by Prussia, Russia and Austria in the 18th century.

The decision to move against the crucifixes came at time of relative calm in Poland. The Solidarity free trade-union movement that was at the center of national turmoil has been banned, and the remnant of the organization that went underground has become quiescent. Its former leader Lech Walesa is slipping back into obscurity.

With the demise of Solidarity, the church has once again become Poland's only national institution capable of championing the people's interests in confrontations with the government. Yet it has become increasingly clear that the church, at least at the top rungs of its hierarchy, is in no mood for conflict, despite the activities of some young activist priests.

The Polish Primate Cardinal Jozef Glemp has repeatedly appealed for calm and patience in dealing with Poland's massive economic, political and social problems. It is an appeal that has echoed throughout the years of communist rule. Whenever the people erupted in anger and frustration over official bungling, the regime pleaded for calm and understanding.

Such an appeal could only become effective with the cooperation or at least quiescence of the church. As the Polish episcopate put it, any challenge to the church leads to social unrest, so why antagonize it unnecessarily?

Thus it seems incomprehensible that the government would decide, as it did last December, to invoke a law—a 23-year-old law—governing the separation of church and state and order the removal of religious objects from state facilities.

Most administrators discreetly ignored the order, but not Ryszard Dobrynski, director of the Staszic school. He repeatedly removed crosses from the school only to find them repeatedly replaced by ones brought by protesting students.

This cycle of action and reaction soon mushroomed into a major confrontation that spread to other schools and inflamed the feelings of Poles throughout the country.

The confrontation erupted while Glemp was on a visit to South America. He immediately joined in the dispute upon his return and, in a sermon, asked rhetorically: "Whom is this cross disturbing so much? Is the law right that sweepingly and rather deeply hurts the feelings of the majority of the believing society?"

Glemp's denunciations were seen as a favorable contrast to what a growing number of critics felt were his overly conciliatory relations with the regime. He had been widely criticized for the recent transfer of Father Mieczyslaw Nowak, an ardent supporter of Solidarity, from his Warsaw church to a remote rural parish.

The confrontation led to intense meetings among church and government leaders, with the church continuing to insist that the crucifixes remain or be restored, while the regime stuck to its position that they must go.

In retrospect, the government may now be wishing that Staszic school director Dobrynski had not been so zealous in carrying out the government ban on crucifixes.

Poland's leader, Gen. Wojciech Jaruzelski, while avoiding public comment on what one bishop called "the war of the crosses," insisted recently that the government seeks no conflict with the church. Yet that is precisely what it got in ordering the removal of the crucifixes. It is no doubt now seeking to find a face-saving solution to a controversy it could have avoided. If so, this latest example of the regime's bungling shows there is not much face left to save.

BIBLIOGRAPHY

An asterisk (*) preceding a reference indicates that the article or part of it has been reprinted in this book.

BOOKS AND PAMPHLETS

Area Handbook for Poland. The American University, Washington, D.C. '73.

Benes, Vaclav and Porends, Norman J. Poland. Westview. '76.

Biddle, A. J. Drexel, Jr., ed. Poland and the coming of the Second World War: diplomatic papers of A. J. Drexel Biddle, Jr. the United States Ambassador to Poland. Ohio State University Press. '76.

Bromke, Adam. Poland's politics: idealism vs. realism. Harvard University Press. '67.

Brumberg, Abraham, ed. Poland: genesis of a revolution. Random House. '83.

Checinski, Michael. Poland: communism, nationalism, anti-Semitism. Karz-Cohl Publishers. '82.

Cieplak, Tadeusz N., ed. Poland since 1956: Readings and essays on Polish government and politics. Irvington. '72.

Davies, Norman. Poland past and present: select bibliography of works in English. Orient Res Partners. '76.

Dobbs, M. and others. Poland-Solidarity-Walesa. McGraw-Hill. '81.

Dziewanowski, M. K. Poland in the 20th century. Columbia University Press. '77.

Goodhart, Arthur L. Poland and the minority races. Arno. '70.

Gronowski, T. and Gronoswska, R. Poland. Heinman. '77.

Heine, Marc. Poland. Hippocrene Books. '80.

Heymann, Frederick G. Poland and Czechoslovakia. Greenwood. '78.

Johnson, A. Ross and others. East European military establishments: the Warsaw Pact northern tier. Crane. '82.

Johnson, Mike. Poland, Solidarity and self-management. Heretic Books. '82.

Karpinski, Jakub. Countdown: the Polish upheavals of 1956, 1968, 1970, 1976, 1980. Karz-Cohl Publishers. '82.

Michener, James A. Poland. Random House. '83.

Persky, Stan and Flam, Henry, eds. The Solidarity sourcebook. New Star Books. '82.

Portes, Richard. The Polish crisis; western economic policy options. Royal Institute of International Affairs, London. F. '81.

Potel, Jean-Yves. The promise of Solidarity: inside the Polish workers' struggle, 1980–82. Praeger. '82.

Preibisz, Joanna M., ed. Polish dissident publications: an annotated bibliography. Praeger. '82.

Raina, Peter. Independent social movements in Poland. Orbis Books, London. '81.

*Schaufele, William E., Jr. Polish paradox: Communism and national renewal. (Headline Series 256) Foreign Policy Association. O. '81.

Shotwell, James and Laserson, Max M. Poland and Russia, nineteen-nineteen to nineteen forty-five. Greenwood. '76.

Staar, Richard F. Poland, nineteen forty-four to nineteen sixty-two: the Sovietization of a captive people. Greenwood. '75.

Starski, Stanislaw. Class struggle in classless Poland. South End Press. '82.

Summerscale, Peter. The East European predicament: changing patterns in Poland, Czechoslovakia and Romania. St. Martin's Press. '82.

Syrop, Konrad. Poland in perspective. Hale. '82.

Szczypiorski, Andrzej. The Polish ordeal: the view from within. Croom Helm Ltd. (Biblio Distribution Centre, London.) '82.

Taylor, John. Five months with Solidarity: a first-hand report from inside Hotel Morski, Gdansk. Wildwood House, London. '81.

Touraine, Alain and others. Solidarity: the analysis of a social movement; Poland 1980–1981. Cambridge University Press. '83.

United States House. Committee on the Budget. The United States and Poland: a report on the current situation in Poland after the declaration of martial law. Committee Print. Washington, D.C. 20515. '82.

United States House. Committee on Foreign Affairs. Subcommittee on Europe and the Middle East. Developments in Europe, February 1982: hearing, February 9, 1982. U.S. Government Printing Office. Washington D.C. 20515. '82.

United States Senate. Committee on Foreign Relations. Poland: its renewal and a U.S. strategy; a report, October 30, 1981. Committee Print. Washington, D.C. 20510. '81.

United States Senate. Committee on Foreign Relations. Subcommittee on European Affairs. The Polish economy: hearing, January 27, 1982, on the Polish economy and Poland's international debt: implications for United States foreign policy. U.S. Government Printing Office. Washington, D.C. 20510. '82.

Weydenthal, Jan B. de. Poland: Communism adrift. The Washington Papers No. 72. Sage Publications for the Center for Strategic and International Studies, Georgetown University. '79.

Wojna, Ryszard. Poland: the country and its people. International Publications Service. '79.

Woodall, Jean, ed. Policy and politics in contemporary Poland: reform, failure, crisis. St. Martin's Press. '82.

Worth, Richard. Poland: the threat to national renewal. Watts. '82.

Yakowicz, Joseph Vincent. Poland's postwar recovery: economic reconstruction, nationalization, and agrarian reform in Poland after World War II. Exposition. '79.

Zurawski, Joseph W. Poland, the captive satellite: a study in national psychology. Endurance. '62.

PERIODICALS

America. 146:162-3. Mr. 6, '82. The Church: in Poland and elsewhere.

America. 147:103. S. 4-11, '82. The witness of Poland.

America. 147:223-4. O. 23, '82. The seasons of Solidarity.

America. 147:263. N. 6, '82. Learning from Lech Walesa.

America. 148:64. Ja. 29, '83. A false peace, without progress.

America. 149:21. Jl. 9-16, '83. The Church in Poland.

American Scholar. 51:487-94. Autumn '82. Polish intellectuals. S. Baranczak.

Atlantic. 246:6-9+. D. '80. Poland: a weakened Communist Party fights for survival. M. Seeger.

Aviation Week and Space Technology. 116:20-1. Ja. 18, '82. NATO allies' stand on Poland falls short of U.S. position.

Bulletin of the Atomic Scientists. 38:7-8. Mr. '82. Marshall Plan for Poland. A. Prezeworski.

Bulletin of the Atomic Scientists. 38:5-8. My. '82. Rethinking East-West relations. Z. Brezezinski.

Business Week. p 44-5. Je. 7, '82. The generals have the economy at a halt.

Business Week. p 44. Ag. 30, '82. The tinder that could spark new violence in Poland. S. W. Sanders.

Christian Century. 99:411+. Ap. 7, '82. Poland and the peace movement. M. L. Stackhouse.

Christianity Today. 26:16-9. Mr. 5, '82. The plight of Poland: news behind the news.

*Commentary. 73:25-30. Mr. '82. What Poland means. Walter Laqueur.

Commonweal. 110:387-8. Jl. 15, '83. Papal defiance, Polish dilemmas.

*Commonweal. 110:390-2. Jl. 15, '83. The Pope and Poland: and now what? resistance, not rebellion. Thomas E. Bird.

Current Digest of the Soviet Press. 33:4-6. Ja. 13, '82. Jaruzelski's appeal to the Polish people [address declaring state of martial law in Poland]. W. Jaruzelski.

Current Digest of the Soviet Press. 34:10-1+. Mr. 24, '82. Jaruzelski's report to the plenary session of the PUWP (Polish United Workers' Party). W. Jaruzelski.

Current History. 81:371-5+. N. '82. Poland: Quo vadis? A. R. Rachwald.

Department of State Bulletin. 82:27-9. Mr. '82. Current international developments. Alexander M. Haig, Jr.

Department of State Bulletin. 82:32-3. Mr. '82. Poland has not perished. Alexander M. Haig, Jr.

Department of State Bulletin. 82:49-52. Mr. '82. Poland: financial and economic situation.

Department of State Bulletin. 82:37-9. S. '82. The case for sanctions against the Soviet Union. J. L. Buckley.

Department of State Bulletin. 82:11-2. D. '82. Solidarity and U.S. relations with Poland [address, October 9, 1982]. R. Reagan.

Economist. 277:68-9. N. 29, '80. Poland's chamber of economic horrors.

Economist. 278:31-2. Ja. 3, '81. Poland moves to another test of the limits of its freedom.

Economist. 280:23-4. Jl. 11, '81. Hole at the heart of the hope.

Economist. 281:11-2. O. 24, '81. Good Soldier Wojciech.

Economist. 281:19-21. D. 19, '81. How the general put his boot on Poland.

Economist. 282:31-3. Ja. 16, '82. What sort of Poland will be left when martial law ends?

Economist. 286:71-3. F. 12, '83. Poland's economy: General Jaruzelski's cupboard is bare.

*Foreign Affairs. 59:522-39. Ap. '81. Poland and the Soviet imperium. Seweryn Bialer.

Foreign Affairs. 61:292-308. Winter '82/'83. Polish futures, Western options. C. Gati.

Foreign Policy. 41:154-62. Winter '80/'81. Poland: the cliff's edge. A. Bromke.

*Foreign Policy. 46:49-66. Spring '82. Clash over Poland. Dimitri K. Simes.

*Fortune. 104:42-8. S. 7, '81. Poland's economic disaster. Robert Ball.

History Today. 32:23-30. N. '82. Poland's dreams of past glory. N. Davies.

History Today. 32:31-2. N. '82. Polish profiles. R. Frost.

International Affairs.[Moscow]. p 67-76. Ap. '82. The hypocritical intrigues around Poland.

*Los Angeles Times. p IV2. Mr. 25, '84. Polish regime takes on the Church, and regrets it. Harry Trimborn.

Macleans. 95:8. Ja. 25, '82. Skating on diplomacy's thin ice.

Macleans. 95:29. Ja. 25, '82. The allies: deceptive harmony. P. Lewis.

Macleans. 95:36. O. 18, '82. The death of Solidarity. P. Lewis.

Macleans. 95:32. N. 29, '82. Walesa at a crossroads. S. Masterman.

Macleans. 95:14-5. D. 27, '82. Walesa's joyless ride. P. Lewis.

Macleans. 96:25. Ag. 1, '83. A cautious end to military rule. P. Lewis.

Macleans. 96:33. Ag. 29, '83. Walesa unfurls a new protest. S. Masterman.

Monthly Labor Review. 105:43-6. My. '82. Solidarity's proposals for reforming Poland's economy.

Nation. 234:229-32. F. 27, '82. Communism and the left. S. Sontag.

Nation. 234:291-2. Mr. 13, '82. Darkness at noon.

Nation. 234:393-4. Ap. 3, '82. The voices of resistance. G. Moszcz.

Nation. 235:1+. Jl. 3, '82. Solidarity—lest we forget. D. Singer.

Nation. 235:517. N. 20, '82. Sovieticus. S. F. Cohen.

Nation. 235:554-6. N. 27, '82. Solidarity will never die. D. Singer.

Nation. 235:645. D. 18, '82. What went wrong. S. Lens.

Nation. 237:173-6. S. 3-10, '83. How many masses is Poland worth? D. Singer.

National Review. 34:14. Ja. 22, '82. Solidarity and disaster.

National Review. 34:68. Ja. 22, '82. The way to help the Poles. J. P. Roche.

National Review. 34:130-1. F. 5, '82. Germans and Poles. J. P. Roche.

National Review. 34:190-1. F. 19, '82. The Archbishop's anguish. J. P. Roche.

National Review. 34:192. F. 19, '82. The stakes are that big. W. F. Buckley.

National Review. 34:371-2. Ap. 2, '82. Poland and the left. D. K. Mano.

National Review. 34:620–1+. My. 28, '82. Ten years, and a million men: Poland, Russia and the West. J. Hutchinson.

National Review. 35:942. Ag. 5, '83. The Pope in Poland. E. von Kuehnelt-Leddihn.

National Review. 35:960–1. Ag. 5, '83. What was the Pope up to? W. F. Buckley.

New Leader. 65:3–5. Ja. 11, '82. Goodbye Poland, hello summit. M. Hopkins.

New Leader. 65:2, 4–5. N. 1, '82. The U.S. choices in Poland (with editorial comment). M. J. Wolnicki.

New Leader. 65:3–4. D. 27, '82. Jaruzelski's four-hands concerto. C. Garnysz.

New Leader. 66:4–5. Je. 27, '83. The Pope and the General. Andrew J. Glass.

New Republic. 186:10+. Ja. 27, '82. Solidarity night special.

*New Republic. 186:13–5. Ja. 27, '82. Poland and the ghost of Yalta. Ronald Steel.

New Republic. 186:13–4. F. 10, '82. A Panglossian Warsaw. C. Krauthammer.

New Republic. 186:15–7. F. 10, '82. The education of Europe's left. F. O. Giesbert.

New Republic. 186:18–20. F. 10, '82. Liberals against liberty. L. Wieseltier.

New Republic. 186:12–4. Mr. 24, '82. "We can only sit." A. Brumberg.

New Republic. 187:16–8. S. 6, '82. Poland's paralysis. A. Brumberg.

New Republic. 187:9–10. N. 1, '82. Jaruzelski's second coup.

New Republic. 188:14–5. Ap. 18, '83. Specious ceremonies. A. Brumberg and R. T. Davies.

New York Review of Books. 29:21–6. Mr. 18, '82. Poland: the winter war. M. Malia.

New York Review of Books. 29:6. D. 2, '82. The danger in Poland: a letter. G. Konrad.

*New York Times. p E 5. F. 26, '84. Art for politics' sake gets sheltered underground. John Kifner.

*New York Times Magazine. p 39–41+. N. 9, '80. 60 days that shook Poland. John Darnton.

*New York Times Magazine. p 24–9+. Ag. 22, '82. Poland: still defiant. John Darnton.

New York Times Magazine. p 126–8+. D. 5, '82. Diary of Poland's discontent. K. Brandys.

New York Times Magazine. p 22–8+. Ag. 7, '83. The trees of Warsaw: a return to Poland. A. M. Rosenthal.

New Yorker. 58:106–8+. Letter from Europe. J. Kramer.

Newsweek. 99:37–8. Ja. 25, '82. Life under Jaruzelski's law. B. Quint.

Newsweek. 99:41–2. F. 1, '82. Recipe for a stalemate. S. Strasser.

Newsweek. 99:47. F. 1, '82. The voice of martial law (excerpts from interview with J. Urban). D. Stanglin.

Newsweek. 99:51. F. 8, '82. A communist excommunication. K. Rogal.

Newsweek. 99:70. F. 8, '82. The Polish dilemma. L. C. Thurow.

Newsweek. 99:36+. Mr. 1, '82. Warsaw's Operation Calm. A. Deming.

Newsweek. 99:41–2. Mr. 8, '82. Jaruzelski's divided party. M. Whitaker.

Newsweek. 99:44. My. 24, '82. A nervous regime seeks scapegoats. J. Brecher.

Newsweek. 100:47. O. 18, '82. Snuffing out Solidarity. J. Brecher.

Newsweek. 100:44–5. O. 25, '82. Solidarity runs for cover. R. Watson.

Newsweek. 100:66. N. 29, '82. Walesa walks the tightrope. J. LeMoyne.

Newsweek. 100:112. D. 13, '82. How soon we forget. M. Greenfield.

Newsweek. 100:48. D. 20, '82. What to do about sanctions. M. Whitaker.

Newsweek. 100:49. D. 20, '82. A Polish agent in place. D. C. Martin.

Newsweek. 101:40. Mr. 21, '83. Walesa: a return to the barricades?

Newsweek. 102:30–1. Jl. 11, '83. Has Walesa been dumped? R. Watson.

Newsweek. 102:37–8. Ag. 1, '83. Martial law is over, but . . . F. Willey.

Newsweek. 102:33. Ag. 29, '83. A heavy blue pencil for the writers' union.

Newsweek. 102:53. S. 12, '83. Sad times for Solidarity. F. Willey.

Orbis. 25:233–46. Spring, '81. Poland, the permanent crisis. F. S. Larrabee.

Problems of Communism. 30:25–39. S./O. '81. Poland today and Czechoslovakia 1968. David W. Paul and Maurice D. Simon.

Progressive. 46:22–5. Mr. '82. Second act in the second world. S. Lens.

Progressive. 47:25–8. F. '83. The road not taken: can Poland steer a middle course? P. Bernstein.

Readers Digest. 120:70–1. Mr. '82. Inside the people's Poland. John Darnton.

Rolling Stone. p 14–16. F. 18, '82. Of Jews and martial law. P. Hellman.

Science. 216:966. My. 28, '82. Poland, United States exchange expulsions. J. Walsh.

Senior Scholastic. 114:19. Ja. 22, '82. Poland: new year, new uncertainties.

Society. 19:36–50. Mr./Ap. '82. The Polish crisis and the Communist malaise. Z. A. Walaszek.

Time. 119:46+. F. 1, '82. Did Solidarity push too hard? T. A. Sancton.

Time. 119:26+. F. 15, '82. Tightening belts at gunpoint. T. A. Sancton.

Time. 119:24–5. F. 22, '82. Good friends—sort of. R. Hoyle.

Time. 119:45–6. Mr. 22, '82. The long night of martial law.

Time. 119:44–6. My. 17, '82. A risky spring offensive. P. Blake.

Time. 120:29+. Jl. 26, '82. The standoff in Victory Square. G. H. Wierzynski.

Time. 120:35. Ag. 30, '82. Recalling in sorrow and hope. J. Kihan.

Time. 120:50. N. 1, '82. Bloodied but still unbowed.

Time. 120:76–7. N. 22, '82. An unwinnable game. J. Kelly.

Time. 121:64–5. Ja. 3, '83. The ideals of Solidarity remain. R. Hornik.

Time. 122:16. Ag. 1, '83. The appearance of change.

USA Today. 110:9+. Mr. '82. Winter in Poland. J. H. Wolfe.

U.S. News & World Report. 91:5–7. D. 28, '81/Ja. 4, '82. Poland's tragedy: when brute force took over.

U.S. News & World Report. 91:7. D. 28, '81/Ja. 4, '82. Resort to force "won't solve any problem" for Kremlin [interview with Walter Laqueur].

U.S. News & World Report. 92:14–6. Ja. 11, '82. Another lost cause for the U.S.? the cards are stacked heavily against Reagan's go-it-alone strategy in the Polish crisis. Joseph Fromm.

U.S. News & World Report. 92:17–8. Ja. 11, '82. How to keep Poland from being "just another historical tragedy" [interview with Zbigniew Brzezinski].

U.S. News & World Report. 92:32. Ja. 25, '82. Despite crackdown in Poland, the human spirit remains [interview with C. Milosz].

U.S. News & World Report. 92:8. F. 22, '82. U.S., allies close ranks on Poland.

*U.S. News & World Report. 92:33–4. Mr. 29, '82. As last hopes for freedom dwindle in Poland. Robin Knight.

U.S. News & World Report. 92:17. My. 17, '82. What happens when Poland lifts its lid.

U.S. News & World Report. 93:11. S. 13, '82. Violence in Poland—more to come?

U.S. News & World Report. 93:39+. D. 20, '82. In Poland, no real easing of regime's grip. S. Powell.

U.S. News & World Report. 95:6. Jl. 11, '83. Behind the Pope's Warsaw pact.

U.S. News & World Report. 95:7. Ag. 1, '83. As U.S. sizes up the new Poland—

Vital Speeches of the Day. 48:485–8. Je. 1, '82. United States foreign policy. L. Kirkland.

Wall Street Journal. 198:1+. D. 29, '81. Divided allies: Bonn-Washington tie is strained by discord over views on Poland. American outrage contrasts over German inaction. John M. Geddes and others.

Wall Street Journal. 198:20. D. 29, '81. The Reagan response on Poland. Seymour Weiss.

Wall Street Journal. 199:24. Ja. 6, '82. Poland: an internal crisis? Arthur J. Goldberg.

Wall Street Journal. 198:1+. Ja. 19, '82. Secular ministry: Polish Catholic Church assumes unifying role with Warsaw's assent; communists rely on stature enjoyed by clerics, who preach against violence. Frederick Kempe.

Wall Street Journal. 199:1+. Mr. 31, '82. Warsaw spring: Poles gloomily accept martial law regime, but it is paying a price. Frederick Kempe.

*Wall Street Journal. 202:1+. Ag. 8, '83. Silesian gold: Poland counts on coal to cure economic ills, but obstacles remain. Frederick Kempe.

*Wall Street Journal. 203:35. F. 1, '84. In Poland, a divided Communist party debates how to make its ideology work. Victoria Pope.

Wilson Quarterly. 7:86–7. Spring '83. Background books.